my revision notes

AQA AS and A-level History

THE TUDORS

England 1485–1603

Roger Turvey

Series editor
David Ferriby

HODDER
EDUCATION
AN HACHETTE UK COMPANY

Acknowledgements

The Publishers would like to thank the following for permission to reproduce copyright material.

p.75 © Susan Doran/BBC History Magazine.

Every effort has been made to trace all copyright holders, but if any have been inadvertently overlooked, the Publishers will be pleased to make the necessary arrangements at the first opportunity.

Although every effort has been made to ensure that website addresses are correct at time of going to press, Hodder Education cannot be held responsible for the content of any website mentioned in this book. It is sometimes possible to find a relocated web page by typing in the address of the home page for a website in the URL window of your browser.

Hachette UK's policy is to use papers that are natural, renewable and recyclable products and made from wood grown in sustainable forests. The logging and manufacturing processes are expected to conform to the environmental regulations of the country of origin.

Orders: please contact Bookpoint Ltd, 130 Milton Park, Abingdon, Oxon OX14 4SE. Telephone: +44 (0)1235 827720. Fax: +44 (0)1235 400454. Email education@bookpoint.co.uk Lines are open from 9 a.m. to 5 p.m., Monday to Saturday, with a 24-hour message answering service. You can also order through our website: www.hoddereducation.co.uk

ISBN: 978 1 4718 7610 3

© Roger Turvey 2016

First published in 2016 by

Hodder Education,
An Hachette UK Company
Carmelite House
50 Victoria Embankment
London EC4Y 0DZ

www.hoddereducation.co.uk

Impression number   10 9 8 7 6 5 4 3 2 1

Year   2020 2019 2018 2017 2016

Cover photo © Nigel Spooner / Alamy Stock Photo
Illustrations by Integra
Typeset by Integra Software Services Pvt. Ltd., Pondicherry, India
Printed in India

A catalogue record for this title is available from the British Library.

My Revision Planner

REVISED

Introduction

Component 1: breadth study

Component 1 involves the study of significant developments over an extended period of time (around 50 years at AS and 100 years at A-level) and an evaluation of historical interpretations.

The Tudors: England 1485–1603

The specification lists the content of Tudor England in two parts, each part being divided into two sections.

Part 1 Consolidation of the Tudor dynasty: England 1485–1547
  1 Henry VII, 1485–1509
  2 Henry VIII and the Royal Supremacy, 1509–47
Part 2 England: turmoil and triumph 1547–1603
  3 Instability and consolidation: the 'mid-Tudor crisis', 1547–63
  4 The triumph of Elizabeth, 1563–1603

Although each period of study is set out in chronological sections in the specification, an exam question may arise from one or more of these sections.

The AS examination

The AS examination which you may be taking includes all the content in Part 1.

You are required to answer:
● Section A: one question on two contrasting interpretations: which is the more convincing? You need to identify the arguments in each extract and assess how convincing they are, using your knowledge, and then reach a judgement on which is the more convincing. The question is worth 25 marks.
● Section B: one essay question out of two. The questions will be set on a broad topic reflecting that this is a breadth paper, and will require you to analyse whether you agree or disagree with a statement. Almost certainly, you will be doing both and reaching a balanced conclusion. The question is worth 25 marks.

The exam lasts one and a half hours, and you should spend about equal time on each section. At AS, Component 1 will be worth a total of 50 marks and 50 per cent of the AS examination.

The A-level examination

The A-level examination at the end of the course includes all the content of Part 1 **and** Part 2.

You are required to answer:
● Section A: one question on three interpretations: how convincing is each interpretation? You are NOT required to reach a conclusion about which might be the most convincing. You need to identify the arguments in each extract and use your knowledge to assess how convincing each one is. The question is worth 30 marks.
● Section B: two essay questions out of three. The questions will be set on a broad topic (usually covering 20–25 years). The question styles will vary, but they will all require you to analyse factors and reach a conclusion. The focus may be on causation, or consequence, or continuity and change. Each question in this section is worth 25 marks.

The exam lasts for two and a half hours. You should spend about one hour on Section A and about 45 minutes on each of the two essays. At A-level, Component 1 will be worth a total of 80 marks and 40 per cent of the A-level.

In both the AS and A-level examinations you are being tested on your ability to:
● use relevant historical information (Sections A and B)
● evaluate different historical interpretations (Section A)
● analyse factors and reach a judgement (Section B).

How to use this book

This book has been designed to help you develop the knowledge and skills necessary to succeed in the examination.

- The book is divided into four sections – one for each section of the A-level specification.
- Each section is made up of a series of topics organised into double-page spreads.
- On the left-hand page you will find a summary of the key content you will need to learn.
- Words in bold in the key content are defined in the glossary (see pages 100–102).
- On the right-hand page you will find exam-focused activities.

Together, these two strands of the book will provide you with the knowledge and skills essential for examination success.

▼ **Key historical content**

▼ **Exam-focused activities**

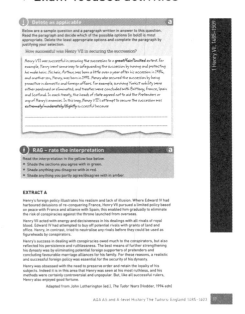

Examination activities

There are three levels of exam-focused activities:

- Band 1 activities are designed to develop the foundation skills needed to pass the exam. These have a green heading and this symbol.
- Band 2 activities are designed to build on the skills developed in Band 1 activities and to help you to achieve a C grade. These have an orange heading and this symbol.
- Band 3 activities are designed to enable you to access the highest grades. These have a purple heading and this symbol.

Some of the activities have answers or suggested answers on pages 104–108. These have the following symbol to indicate this.

Each section ends with an exam-style question and sample answers with commentary. This will give you guidance on what is expected to achieve the top grade.

You can also keep track of your revision by ticking off each topic heading in the book, or by ticking the checklist on the contents page. Tick each box when you have:

- revised and understood a topic
- completed the activities.

Mark schemes

For some of the activities in the book it will be useful to refer to the mark schemes for this paper. Below are abbreviated forms.

Section A Interpretations

Level	AS-level exam	A-level exam
1	Unsupported vague or general comments. Little understanding of the interpretations. (1–5)	Mostly general or vague comments OR shows an accurate understanding of one extract only. (1–6)
2	Partial understanding of the interpretations. Undeveloped comments with a little knowledge. (6–10)	Some accurate comments on interpretations given in at least two of the extracts. Some analysis, but little evaluation. (7–12)
3	Reasonable understanding of interpretations. Some knowledge to support arguments. (11–15)	Some supported comments on the three interpretations, with comments on strength, with some analysis and evaluation. (13–18)
4	Good understanding of interpretations. A supported conclusion, but not all comments well-substantiated and judgements may be limited. (16–20)	Good understanding of the interpretations, combined with knowledge of historical context, with mostly well-supported evaluation, but with minor limitations in depth and breadth. (19–24)
5	Good understanding of interpretations. Thorough evaluation of extracts leading to a well-substantiated judgement. (21–25)	Very good understanding of interpretations, combined with strong awareness of historical context to analyse and evaluate with well-supported arguments. (25–30)

Section B Essays

Level	AS-level exam	A-level exam
1	Extremely limited or irrelevant information. Unsupported, vague or generalist comments. (1–5)	Extremely limited or irrelevant information. Unsupported, vague or generalist comments. (1–5)
2	Descriptive or partial, failing to grasp full demands of question. Limited in scope. (6–10)	Descriptive or partial, failing to grasp full demands of question. Limited in scope. (6–10)
3	Some understanding and answer is adequately organised. Information showing understanding of some key features. (11–15)	Understanding of question and a range of largely accurate information showing awareness of key issues and features, but lacking in precise detail. Some balance established. (11–15)
4	Understanding shown, with range of largely accurate information showing awareness of some of the key issues and features leading to a limited judgement. (16–20)	Good understanding of question. Well-organised and effectively communicated, with range of clear and specific supporting information showing good understanding of key features and issues, with some conceptual awareness. (16–20)
5	Good understanding. Well-organised and effectively communicated. Range of clear information showing good understanding and some conceptual awareness. Analytical in style, leading to a substantiated judgement. (21–25)	Very good understanding of full demands of question. Well-organised and effectively delivered, with well-selected, precise supporting information. Fully analytical, with balanced argument and well-substantiated judgement. (21–25)

1 Henry VII, 1485–1509

Henry Tudor's consolidation of power: character, aims and establishing the Tudor dynasty

REVISED

Claim to the throne

Henry Tudor's claim to the throne was weak.

- Henry's claim came through his mother, Margaret Beaufort, who was a direct descendant of Edward III by the marriage of his third son, John of Gaunt, Duke of Lancaster, to Katherine Swynford. However, the fact that John and Katherine's son, John Beaufort (Margaret's grandfather), had been born prior to their marriage weakened any future claim to the throne by this line of descent.
- Henry inherited royal blood from his father, Edmund Tudor. Edmund's French mother, Catherine, had been married to Henry V before she became the wife of Edmund's Welsh father, Owen. Edmund was the half-brother of the king, Henry VI. Henry VI raised his half-brother to the peerage by creating Edmund, Earl of Richmond. Therefore, Henry VII was the half-nephew of the king of England and a member of the extended royal family.
- In reality, Henry's claim to the throne rested on his victory in battle. That he had defeated and killed king Richard III was regarded as a sign that God had approved of Henry's assumption of power.

Aims

Henry VII's aim was to remain king and establish his dynasty by handing on an unchallenged succession to his descendants. His policies at home and abroad were shaped and dictated by this aim. Therefore, his goals were simple: to secure and strengthen his dynasty. He knew that if he was to prove himself a strong king and retain full control of his realm he would have to:

- establish effective government
- maintain law and order
- control the nobility
- secure the Crown's finances.

He would also need good advice, friends abroad and a considerable amount of luck.

Character

The character of the king was important because the ruler was responsible for policy and was closely involved in the business of government. Because monarchy was personal, everything depended on the monarch's energy, interest and willingness to work.

Historians have been more concerned with Henry's aims and achievements than his character, which explains why they tend to disagree about what he was like.

Establishing and consolidating the Tudor dynasty

- Henry dated the beginning of his reign from the day before the battle of **Bosworth**: 22 August 1485. Therefore Richard and his supporters could be declared traitors, which meant that their estates became the property of the Crown by Act of Attainder.
- Henry deliberately arranged his coronation before the first meeting of parliament. Thus it could never be said that parliament made him king.
- He married Elizabeth of York, the daughter of Edward IV. This united the Houses of Lancaster and York and dissuaded many Yorkists from challenging Henry.
- The birth of a son and heir, Arthur, early in the reign (September 1486) helped to establish the dynasty (see page 16).
- Henry enlisted the support of the Church and gained control of the nobility (see page 12).
- He secured the support of the Pope and the kings of France and Spain, who recognised the legitimacy of his kingship (see page 14).

Quick quizzes at **www.hoddereducation.co.uk/myrevisionnotes**

! Spot the mistake a

Below are a sample question and a paragraph written in answer to this question. Why does this paragraph not get high praise? What is wrong with the focus of the answer in this paragraph?

To what extent do you agree that Henry VII's claim to the throne was weak?

Henry's claim to the throne was weak because his father was an earl and not a king. His grandfather was not even an Englishman; he was a Welsh squire. Henry's claim through inheritance was weak because it descended through the female line. Henry was an exiled earl who took a gamble on winning the throne by invading England and facing Richard III in battle.

Support or challenge? a

Below is a sample question which asks to what extent you agree with a specific statement. The table sets out a list of general statements that are relevant to the question. Using your own knowledge and the information on the opposite page, decide whether these statements support or challenge the statement in the question.

Do you agree that the main reason Henry VII succeeded in establishing the dynasty was due to the strength of his royal connections?

	SUPPORT	CHALLENGE
Henry VII was descended from Edward III		
Henry VII was a hard-working and energetic monarch		
Henry VII was the half-nephew of Henry VI		
Henry VII had the support of the Pope and the Church		
Henry VII controlled the nobility		
Henry VII married Elizabeth, the daughter of Edward IV		

Government: councils, parliament and justice

Central government

The centre of medieval English government was the king himself and the men he chose to sit on his council. The functions of the **king's council** were to advise the king on matters of state, to administer law and order, and to control local government.

Henry relied on a small, core group of councillors who met with him regularly. This elite group included the chief officers of state, which gave stability to the new regime.

To improve the efficiency of central government, Henry decided to use smaller committees formed from within the council.
- One committee took responsibility for the implementation of the Acts of **livery and maintenance**.
- Another, the **Court of General Surveyors**, audited the revenues from Crown lands.
- The **Council Learned in the Law** was responsible for **wardship**, marriage and relief of all the king's tenants, and the collection of **feudal dues**. This Council was disliked because of its connection with **bonds and recognisances**. By the end of the reign it had become the most detested, but the most important, of all Henry's institutions of government.

Regional government

The government of the kingdom was entrusted to key men appointed by the king to govern through regional councils. Henry VII did this because he trusted these men to follow his orders without question:
- Thomas Howard, Earl of Surrey   Council of the North
- Jasper Tudor, Duke of Bedford   Council in Wales and the Marches
- Sir Edward Poyning   Council of Ireland

Local government

The key unit of local government was the county. The sheriff and the **Justice of the Peace** (JP) were the two most important royal officials in each county. JPs were appointed to the commission of the peace for life; sheriffs were selected annually.

The sheriffs were the Crown's representatives in every county throughout England and were responsible for:
- the management of parliamentary elections
- peacekeeping and the detention of criminals.

JPs governed and dispensed justice in courts known as **quarter sessions**. Here they had the power to:
- arrest, try and imprison
- issue a range of punishments, including the death penalty.

Serious offences such as treason and rebellion were tried at the **courts of assize**, presided over by judges appointed by the Crown. The highest criminal court was the **Court of king's Bench**, which could override decisions made at the quarter sessions and assize courts.

Parliament

Parliament was summoned on seven occasions, and five of those were in Henry's first decade as king, when he was relatively insecure. The government bills most frequently passed were **Acts of Attainder**, designed to subdue his political opponents.

Legislation was also used to carry out his policies against riots and **retaining**, and 10 per cent of all statutes dealt with the responsibilities of the JPs and the control of the provinces. Further acts dealt with social discipline, such as that of 1495, which laid down rules on wages and hours of work. Henry's limited use of parliament, especially after 1495, when he only called it twice, emphasised the fact that all power derived from the Crown.

Mind map

Use the information on the opposite page to add detail to the mind map below to show how the different parts of government helped Henry VII to govern the kingdom.

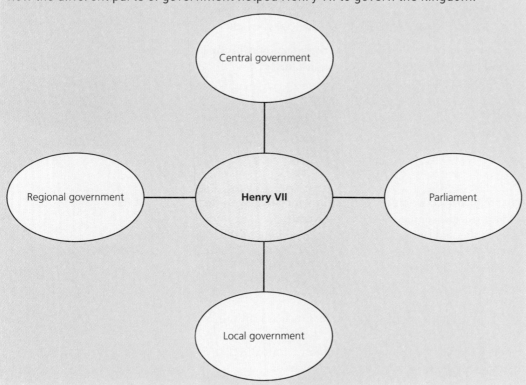

Spectrum of importance a

Below is a sample AS-level question and a list of general points that could be used to answer the question. Use your own knowledge and the information on the opposite page to reach a judgement about the importance of these general points to the question posed.

Write numbers on the spectrum below to indicate their relative importance. Having done this, write a brief justification of your placement, explaining why some of these factors are more important than others. The resulting diagram could form the basis of an essay plan.

'Henry VII's success in government was due to the elite group of councillors who advised him in the king's council.' Explain why you agree or disagree with this view.

1 Work and advice of the elite group of councillors in the king's council

2 The effectiveness of the Council Learned in the Law

3 The key men entrusted with responsibility for the regional councils

4 The work of the sheriffs and the Justices of the Peace

5 Bonds and recognisances and laws against retaining

6 Henry VII

Least important   Most important

Royal finance and domestic policies

Royal finance

Henry VII's financial aims were quite simple: to achieve solvency by increasing royal income, decreasing expenditure and thereby restoring the Crown's financial strength.

Henry did not feel secure unless he was rich, which helps to explain why his financial administration was ruthlessly efficient. He could use his wealth to:

- reward loyal service
- bribe potential opponents
- fund armies
- consolidate the dynasty: a full treasury would provide his heir with the resources to fight to retain the throne.

Ordinary revenue

Ordinary revenue was the regular income on which the Crown could rely to finance the costs of monarchy. There were four principal sources of ordinary revenue:

- Crown lands consisted of inherited lands that included the Earldoms of Richmond, March and Warwick, the Duchy of Lancaster and the Principality of Wales. The annual income from Crown lands increased from £29,000 in 1485 to £42,000 in 1509.
- Customs duties provided a third of the Crown's ordinary revenue. The average annual receipts rose from £33,000 to around £40,000.
- Feudal dues: in 1487 the annual proceeds from feudal dues such as wardship and marriage was £350, but by 1507 this had risen to £6,000.
- Legal system and profits of justice: Henry ensured that most criminal acts, including treason, were punished by fines rather than by imprisonment or execution.

Extraordinary revenue

Extraordinary revenue was money that came to the Crown on particular occasions and therefore with no regularity. There were six principal sources of extraordinary revenue:

- Bonds and recognisances: the practice of subjects paying a sum of money to the Crown as a guarantee of their future good behaviour. Receipts rose from £3,000 in 1493 to £35,000 in 1505.
- Clerical taxes: grants made by **Convocation**, such as the £25,000 towards the cost of the French campaign of 1491–92.
- Feudal obligations: the right to levy such obligations as **distraint of knighthood** or to demand payment for special occasions, such as the marriage of his eldest daughter.
- French pension: the king of France promised (Treaty of Étaples, 1492) to pay Henry £159,000 in annual instalments of £5,000.
- Loans and benevolences: requests made to his landholding subjects for financial support that were virtually impossible to decline, even though they were traditionally in the form of 'agreements'.
- Parliamentary grants: raised by means of taxes on moveable property called 'fifteenths' and 'tenths'. These helped pay for the battle of Stoke that marked the defeat of the Yorkists and the French campaign.

Domestic policies

Henry's financial administration underpinned and supported his other domestic policies, which were geared towards controlling the nobility, co-operating with the Church and maintaining law and order.

- Nobility: controlled the nobility by issuing attainders, curbing retaining and rewarding good service.
- Church: Henry offered the Church his patronage and protection and it publicly upheld his God-given right to rule. The head of the Church, the Pope, supported Henry.
- Law and order: agents of central government such as JPs and sheriffs, supported by trusted noble governors working through regional councils, brought the kingdom under control.

! Spot the mistake · a

Below are a sample question and a paragraph written in answer to this question. Why does this paragraph not get high praise? What is wrong with the focus of the answer in this paragraph?

> To what extent do you agree that Henry VII's financial policies made the most important contribution to his success as a ruler?

> Henry VII's success as a ruler was due almost entirely to the way he ruthlessly exploited and developed the kingdom's revenue system. He bullied the nobility into submission and bribed the Church into supporting him. Henry defeated rival claimants to the throne and eliminated threats to his power from within. Henry VII believed that the wealth gained from making the kingdom solvent would secure his position and establish his dynasty.

! Interpretations: content or argument? · a

Read the interpretation in Extract A at the bottom of the page and the two alternative answers to the question below.

Which answer focuses more on the content and which focuses more on the arguments of the interpretation? Explain your choice.

> Using your understanding of the historical context, assess how convincing the arguments in this extract are in relation to an analysis of the success of Henry VII's financial policies.

Answer 1

> This extract states that Henry VII's financial policy was a success because he was solvent by 1490. Henry's investments had paid off because he was able to leave his heir with a large fortune in cash and thousands of pounds worth of plate and jewels. There is no doubt that Henry's financial policy was one of his major achievements.

Answer 2

> This extract argues that Henry VII successfully restored the Crown's finances. That a near bankrupt kingdom had become solvent in little over five years is a measure of Henry's success in managing the Crown's finances. This is considered to be one of Henry VII's most significant achievements because he was the first king in a century to achieve solvency. However, it is important to put the success of his financial policy into perspective. Henry bequeathed his heir a modest fortune, and in spite of his success England was still poor in comparison to its European neighbours, France and Spain.

EXTRACT A

By about 1490 Henry was solvent. It was rumoured that he left a substantial fortune for his heir to squander, but in fact the [treasury] contained only £9,000 in cash at the time of his death. There may have been other, unrecorded, sums in the hands of [royal officials], and the plate and jewels in which Henry had invested were worth many thousands of pounds, but even when these are taken into account they do not add up to a 'fortune'. Recognition of Henry VII's undoubted and major achievement in restoring the royal finances must not, therefore, obscure the fundamental truth that by European standards the English monarchy was under-endowed, circumscribed in its freedom of action, and dependent upon a considerable degree of co-operation – however grudgingly given – from those who were subject to it.

Adapted from R. Lockyer, *Henry VII* (Longman, 1983)

Relationships with Scotland, France, Spain and other foreign powers

Henry VII's relationship with foreign powers

Henry's vulnerable position in dynastic and financial terms made non-intervention on the Continent the most sensible approach. Henry's foreign policy was subordinated to his domestic policies of enriching the monarchy and ensuring the obedience of his subjects.

Henry's actions in foreign affairs were designed to give him time to consolidate support. He had to ensure he had support abroad if he was to secure his throne at home. Dynastic threats dominated his dealings with foreign rulers, which is why the issue of security lay at the heart of the treaties he concluded with France, Spain, Scotland and Brittany. By 1508 Henry had achieved a measure of stability in his foreign relations and his position on the throne was secure from foreign intervention.

Scotland

The most vulnerable land border was the northern one with Scotland. Scotland was England's traditional enemy, made more dangerous because of the Scots' 'auld alliance' with France.

Relations between Scotland and England were always tense, but when James IV of Scotland offered **Perkin Warbeck** his support in 1495, the prospect of war seemed imminent. However, James lost faith in Warbeck and decided instead to come to terms with Henry. The truce of Ayton was concluded in 1497, becoming a full treaty of peace in 1502. The treaty was sealed in 1503 by the marriage of James IV to Henry's daughter, Margaret.

Spain

The most significant achievement of Henry VII's foreign policy was the alliance negotiated with Spain in the Treaty of Medina del Campo in 1489. It was agreed that Henry's heir, Prince Arthur, would marry Ferdinand and Isabella's youngest daughter, **Catherine of Aragon**. The Tudor dynasty had been recognised as an equal by one of the leading royal families of Europe. This was of major importance to a usurper who was keen to secure international recognition of the legitimacy of his kingship.

France

Relations between France and England had been harmonious, but this changed when France threatened the independence of Brittany. Henry announced his intention to assert his claim to the French Crown and in 1492 sent an army across the Channel, where it laid siege to Boulogne. Charles VIII of France wished to avoid war and agreed to sign the Treaty of Étaples in 1492. Charles promised not to give any aid to English rebels, particularly Warbeck, to pay most of Henry's campaign costs and to pay an annual pension of some £5,000, approximately 5 per cent of Henry's annual income.

Brittany and Burgundy

To support Breton independence, Henry signed the Treaty of Redon in 1489. However, his attempt to prevent France from annexing Brittany failed.

Burgundy provided the greatest threat to Henry because Edward IV's sister, Margaret, was married to the ruler. Margaret supported the Pretenders, **Lambert Simnel** (1487) and Warbeck, with finance and mercenary troops. She also threatened the important English cloth industry because Burgundy was a major trading partner of England. Burgundy ceased to be a threat after Margaret's death in 1503.

! Complete the paragraph

Below are a sample question and a paragraph written in answer to this question. The paragraph contains a point and specific examples, but lacks a concluding analytical link back to the question. Complete the paragraph, adding this link back to the question in the space provided.

How successful was Henry VII's foreign policy?

Henry's foreign policy was careful, measured and was subordinated to his primary aims of securing and maintaining his kingship of England. Henry did not have the money to fight wars, which is why he followed a largely non-interventionist foreign policy. Where possible, he avoided antagonising his continental neighbours, preferring instead to encourage friendship by concluding treaties and alliances. However, Henry was not prepared to tolerate any foreign power threatening his security by supporting or funding rival claimants, such as the Pretenders, Simnel and Warbeck. Overall,

_____

_____

♦ RAG – rate the timeline   a

Below are a sample question and a timeline. Read the question, study the timeline and, using three coloured pens, put a red, amber or green star next to the events to show:

● Red: events and policies that have no relevance to the question
● Amber: events and policies that have some significance to the question
● Green: events and policies that are directly relevant to the question.

How far do you agree that Henry VII's foreign policy made a significant contribution to achieving his aim of securing the throne?

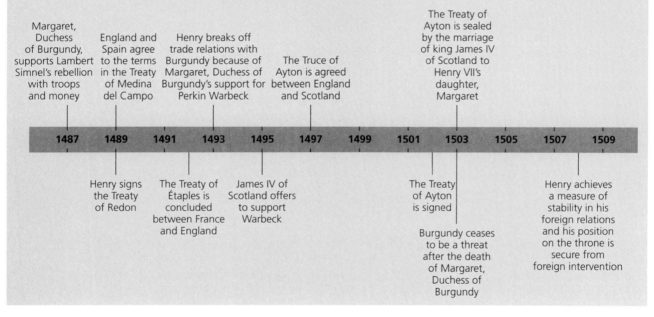

Securing the succession and marriage alliances

Securing the succession

Henry's chief priority was securing the succession. To do this he had to secure the kingdom at home and find allies abroad. To safeguard the succession, Henry had to have and protect a male heir. His heir, Arthur, was born a little over year after his accession in 1486, and another son, Henry, was born in 1491. To establish a dynasty and ensure continuity of succession, Henry's sons would need to marry and have children of their own. To promote the Tudor dynasty, Henry sought suitable brides from among Europe's royal families. Marriage alliances negotiated by treaty would help to ensure the Tudor succession.

Securing the succession at home

In 1485 there were still a number of important Yorkists alive with a strong claim to the throne:
● **Edward, Earl of Warwick**
● **John de la Pole, Earl of Lincoln**.

The 10-year-old Warwick was sent to the Tower of London. He remained in comfortable confinement until 1499, when he was executed for conspiring with Perkin Warbeck to escape from the Tower.

Lincoln was invited to join the government and became a member of the king's council. He remained loyal until the spring of 1487, when he fled the court and joined the Pretender Lambert Simnel. Lincoln was killed at the battle of Stoke in June 1487.

Surviving Yorkist nobility were either pardoned or eliminated:
● Thomas Howard, Earl of Surrey and Henry Percy, Earl of Northumberland were pardoned. They could prove useful and were prepared to work with the new regime.
● Francis, Lord Lovell, Humphrey and Sir Thomas Stafford and Edmund de la Pole, Earl of Suffolk were executed. They were unwilling to work with the new king and so had to be disposed of. This would also set a powerful example to deter other would-be rebels.

Securing the succession abroad

Henry's foreign policy was defensive because of the nature of his succession, by usurpation. There were several claimants to his throne who sought aid from foreign powers and Henry had to be constantly on his guard against possible invasion.

The two claimants who posed the most serious threat to Henry's throne were the Pretenders, Simnel and Warbeck. Henry used diplomacy to conclude treaties with Brittany, France, Spain and Scotland. In each treaty, the heads of state agreed not to aid the Pretenders or any of Henry's enemies, such as the Earl of Suffolk and his brother Richard de la Pole, who fled England for the Continent in 1501.

Marriage alliances

Henry used marriage as a diplomatic device to bind Spain and Scotland into a closer union with England. Sealed by treaty, these marriages helped to secure the succession because the Spanish and Scottish royal families had a personal connection with the Tudor dynasty. It was in their interests to ensure the survival of the Tudors.
● In accordance with the terms of the Treaty of Medina del Campo (1489), Henry's heir, Arthur, was promised in marriage to Catherine of Aragon, daughter of king Ferdinand and Queen Isabella of Spain. When Arthur died in 1502, it was agreed that Catherine would marry Arthur's brother, Henry.
● In accordance with the terms of the Treaty of Ayton (1502), Margaret, Henry VII's eldest daughter, was married to James IV of Scotland in 1503.

Delete as applicable

a

Below are a sample question and a paragraph written in answer to this question. Read the paragraph and decide which of the possible options (in bold) is most appropriate. Delete the least appropriate options and complete the paragraph by justifying your selection.

How successful was Henry VII in securing the succession?

Henry VII was successful in securing the succession to a **great/fair/limited** extent. For example, Henry went some way to safeguarding the succession by having and protecting his male heirs. His heir, Arthur, was born a little over a year after his accession in 1486, and another son, Henry, was born in 1491. Henry also secured the succession by being proactive in domestic and foreign affairs. For example, surviving Yorkist nobility were either pardoned or eliminated, and treaties were concluded with Brittany, France, Spain and Scotland. In each treaty, the heads of state agreed not to aid the Pretenders or any of Henry's enemies. In this way, Henry VII's attempt to secure the succession was **extremely/moderately/slightly** successful because

_____

_____

RAG – rate the interpretation

a

Read the interpretation in the yellow box below.

- Shade the sections you agree with in green.
- Shade anything you disagree with in red.
- Shade anything you partly agree/disagree with in amber.

EXTRACT A

Henry's foreign policy illustrates his realism and lack of illusion. Where Edward IV had harboured delusions of re-conquering France, Henry VII pursued a limited policy based on peace with France and alliance with Spain; this enabled him gradually to eliminate the risk of conspiracies against the throne launched from overseas.

Henry VII acted with energy and decisiveness in his dealings with all rivals of royal blood. Edward IV had attempted to buy off potential rivals with grants of land and office. Henry, in contrast, tried to neutralise any rivals before they could be used as figureheads by conspirators.

Henry's success in dealing with conspiracies owed much to the conspirators, but also reflected his persistence and ruthlessness. The best means of further strengthening his dynasty was by eliminating potential foreign supporters of pretenders and concluding favourable marriage alliances for his family. For these reasons, a realistic and successful foreign policy was essential for the security of his dynasty.

Henry was obsessed with the need to preserve order and retain the loyalty of his subjects. Indeed it is in this area that Henry was seen at his most ruthless, and his methods were certainly controversial and unpopular. But, like all successful rulers, Henry also enjoyed good fortune.

Adapted from John Lotherington (ed.), *The Tudor Years* (Hodder, 1994 edn)

Society: churchmen, nobles and commoners

Society

Tudor society was hierarchical and based on a class system. Social status dominated society and a person's place within this social pyramid was strictly observed. At the tip of this pyramid was the king, followed by the nobility, gentry and higher clergy. Next came the merchants, **burgesses**, artisans, lower clergy and yeomen. The base of the pyramid was occupied by the vast majority of the population, the commoners. The commoners consisted of servants, labouring poor and those without work, the paupers and vagrants.

According to the teachings of the Church, each class had a duty to serve those above. By the same token, the higher classes were obliged to look after the interests of those below. This theory of obligation, known as the **Great Chain of Being**, was the natural order of society.

Church and churchmen

The Roman Catholic Church was a large and powerful organisation that consisted of the **regular clergy** – some 10,000 strong – and **secular clergy** – numbering around 35,000. It formed a state within a state, with its own system of law courts and privileges, which rivalled the authority of the king. These courts dealt with religious crimes such as adultery and heresy, and crimes committed by churchmen. There was a vast social and economic gap between the higher or senior clergy – bishops and abbots – and the lower clergy – parish priests and chaplains. Bishops and abbots had a political voice, being entitled to sit in the House of Lords. Archbishops such as **John Morton** and bishops like **Richard Fox** served as royal councillors and advised the king on matters of justice and administration.

Nobility and gentry

The nobility and gentry formed the most privileged class in England. The nobles and gentry were few in number – in 1500 there were 55 nobles, 500 knights, 800 esquires and 5,000 gentlemen – making up just 1 per cent of the population. Their wealth and power derived from substantial landowning and office holding. The Crown relied on this class to govern the kingdom, keep the peace and pay the majority of the kingdom's taxes. Parliament was used as a means to gauge the attitudes and opinions of this class. While all the nobles were entitled to a seat in the House of Lords, the gentry elected members to represent them in the House of Commons.

The commoners

There were just over 2 million commoners living in England and Wales in 1500. Of these, some 50 per cent lived at or below the poverty line. These were the labouring poor, the majority of whom lived and worked in rural areas. A minority of commoners were able either to rent or buy land, which enabled them to rise in economic terms. They were the husbandmen and yeomen. Some yeomen were economically better off than some gentlemen and esquires, but they remained socially inferior. The lines between economic wealth and social division began to blur during the sixteenth century, when there was greater social mobility.

Summarise the arguments

a

Below are a sample question and an extract referred to in the question. You should read the extract and identify the interpretation offered. Look for the arguments of the passage.

> With reference to the extract and your understanding of the historical context, how convincing do you find the extract in relation to the scale of social change during the reign of Henry VII?

Interpretation offered by the extract:

_____

_____

EXTRACT A

As society grew, differences between one class and another narrowed. Men who had acquired wealth through trade or farming built houses and bought lands that were every bit as impressive as those of the traditional aristocracy. 'Emparking' – the consolidation and enclosure of fields to create parkland for country estates – was another sign of new found wealth.

The sixteenth century saw the rise of the gentry class. This was a large, ill-defined group below the titled nobility, but above tenant farmers and small landowners. They were defined more by their personal wealth than by titles. They could be prosperous farmers, wealthy merchants or men from long-standing families of knights, esquires or gentlemen, but all were able to live comfortably from their income without having to resort to working for a living. The expansion of this group helped to cause an obsession with the symbols of rank as those with traditional status tried to protect their elite position.

> From A. Anderson and T. Imperato, _An Introduction to Tudor England, 1485–1603_ (Hodder & Stoughton, 2001)

Eliminate irrelevance

a

Below are a sample question and a paragraph written in answer to this question. Read the paragraph and identify parts of the paragraph that are not directly relevant to the question. Draw a line through the information that is irrelevant and justify your deletions in the margin.

> To what extent is it accurate to say that there were increased opportunities for social mobility during Henry VII's reign?

Early modern English society was structured and governed by strict rules so that everyone knew his or her place. The Church taught that God was responsible for these rules, which were explained in the so-called 'Great Chain of Being'. The different ranks in society were determined by title, wealth and breeding, which made it virtually impossible for members of the lowest rank, the commoners, to improve their social status. However, by developing the economy and promoting the increase in trade, Henry VII provided the means by which enterprising members of the commons could make a fortune. For example, Robert Wolsey, a butcher and cattle dealer from Ipswich, used his wealth by trade to educate and promote the ecclesiastical career of his son, Thomas. Thomas entered the service of Bishop Richard Fox, where he learnt the art of government and administration. Thomas later became Lord Chancellor and one of the most powerful men in England under Henry VIII.

Regional division, social discontent and rebellions

Regional divisions

The regional division of the kingdom of England was marked by councils set up to govern distant and distinct parts of the realm.

- The north of England was governed through the Council of the North based in York.
- Wales and the western counties of England were governed through the Council of Wales and the Marches based in Ludlow.

Outside the kingdom of England, the king ruled Ireland and a small part of France centred on Calais.

- Ireland was governed through the Council of Ireland based in Dublin.
- Calais was governed by a captain appointed by the king.

Regional division was complicated by:

- the existence of semi-independent lordships, which were self-governing units in which the **'king's writ did not run'**; the Crown had limited power in the **Marcher lordships** of Wales and the **County Palatines** of Durham and Chester
- ethnic and racial differences – Wales, Cornwall, Ireland and Calais each had its own language and culture.

Henry's drive to forge stronger links between central and local governments caused friction in these distant regions. Regional loyalties were strong and there was growing resentment at what was regarded as outside interference. The extension of royal government was accompanied by a strengthening of royal justice. Officials appointed by the London-based government were unwelcome in regions where local lords had been passed over in favour of royal nominees.

Social discontent and rebellions

When Henry came to power he was a largely unknown and untried nobleman. Few of his subjects believed that the civil wars were over or that he would remain king for long. The uncertainty of his rule, the continuing political instability and the economic dislocation caused by civil war affected nobleman and commoner alike.

Henry had to deal with the disgruntled protesters against such things as high taxes and food shortages, alongside the dangerous pretenders or rival claimants to the throne. Henry could not afford to ignore or treat lightly any protest or rebellion.

Protest and rebellions in Yorkshire (1489) and Cornwall (1497)

These rebellions stemmed from the king's demands for money. Compared with the prosperous south-east of England, these regions were poor and they could ill-afford to bear the increasing burden of taxation. Social discontent in these regions led to local protests, but because the Crown appeared to be indifferent to their social and economic problems, they turned into rebellion. The economic and social differences between the regions showed how delicate the balance was between public order and lawlessness.

Within England there were great differences between regions, counties and even neighbouring villages. Yorkshire folk resented being taxed and governed by southerners. This antipathy between northerners and southerners was made worse by the fact that this region had been the centre of Yorkist power.

The traditionally independent-minded Cornish refused to contribute to the defence of the northern part of the kingdom. The Scottish border meant nothing to the Cornish and they were unwilling to pay a tax demanded by a distant government based in the south-east of England.

! Use own knowledge to support or contradict

Below is an extract to read. You are asked to summarise the interpretation about the reasons why Henry VII faced rebellions, and then develop a counter-argument.

Interpretation offered by the extract:

_____

_____

Counter-argument:

_____

_____

EXTRACT A

In addition to the Simnel and Warbeck risings, Henry VII also faced other, less serious, rebellions – in Yorkshire in 1489 and in Cornwall in 1497. The 1489 rebellion was sparked by a parliamentary tax, voted to finance Henry's aid to Brittany. Not only had Yorkshire suffered from a particularly bad harvest, but there was also resentment that counties further north did not have to pay the tax. Rebellion in Cornwall in 1497 was also triggered by a demand for money, this time to pay for a campaign to resist a projected invasion by James IV of Scotland and Perkin Warbeck. The Cornish refused to pay because they considered that any invasion threat in the north would have little relevance to them.

Adapted from D. Rogerson, S. Ellsmore and D. Hudson,
The Early Tudors: England, 1485–1558 (John Murray, 2001)

i Develop the detail

Below are a sample question and a paragraph written in answer to this question. The paragraph contains a limited amount of detail. Annotate the paragraph to add additional detail to the answer.

To what extent did regional divisions contribute to social discontent and the outbreak of rebellion?

Regional divisions were complicated by a number of factors, such as the existence of semi-independent and self-governing lordships. The kingdom governed by Henry VII consisted of England, Wales, Ireland and Calais. The ethnic and racial differences were a further complication, as was the fact that the king's subjects spoke a number of different languages, making communication difficult. Even within England itself there were significant differences between northerners, southerners and the people of the far south-west. The wealth enjoyed by southerners was resented by poorer northerners.

Economic development: trade, exploration, prosperity and depression

Economic developments

England was a largely agricultural country in which nearly 90 per cent of its population lived and worked on the land. Arable farming was the mainstay of the agricultural industry, but its dominance was being challenged by the growth of pastoral farming. The most significant economic developments lay in the growth of industry and the expansion of trade. The three most important industries in England at the beginning of the sixteenth century were cloth, coal and iron. The coal and iron industries were small in comparison with the cloth industry, which was by far the biggest in the kingdom. The cloth industry was closely linked to agriculture because it relied on the supply of wool. English cloth was exported to the continent mainly through the city of Antwerp. England's cloth trade with the Netherlands was so significant that it was used as an economic weapon by Henry VII to encourage the Duke of Burgundy to cease his support for Perkin Warbeck.

Trade

Henry VII recognised early on the importance of flourishing trade to a healthy economy, which in turn would strengthen the Tudors' grip on the throne. To expand English trade with other countries, Henry built a merchant fleet that could compete with those of his continental rivals. The **Navigation Acts** (1485–86) were passed in an attempt to promote and protect English trade and thereby break the monopoly enjoyed by the **Hanseatic League**. Henry also supported the Merchant Adventurers, a trading company which controlled the export and sale of English cloth. Trade, and the revenue derived from it in customs duties and taxes, led Henry to insert a clause on trade in every treaty he signed. For example, in 1490, Henry's treaty with Florence enabled English merchants to trade into the Mediterranean. The exploration, discovery and claim to new lands led to greater opportunities to expand trade. Henry believed that wealth derived by trade would promote the security of his dynasty.

Exploration

Henry was keen to follow Spain by encouraging overseas exploration. He patronised adventurers John and Sebastian Cabot, who sailed to North America to explore and claim new lands for the king of England. The waters off Greenland proved especially rich in fish. They were also tasked with discovering a sea route to reach Asia, in order to participate in the spice trade.

Prosperity and depression

The development of industry and the expansion of trade in the Mediterranean and Baltic contributed to significant growth in England's economy. This led to increasing wealth and prosperity. However, expansion was followed by periods of contraction and depression, especially when international political disputes intruded into trade. In 1493, Henry issued a trade embargo against the Netherlands because of its support for Perkin Warbeck. This led to a severe depression in the cloth industry. Prosperity only returned when the embargo ended with the signing of the *Intercursus Magnus* in 1496. This was followed by the *Intercursus Malus* in 1507.

Spot the mistake **a**

Below are a sample question and a paragraph written in answer to this question. Why does this paragraph not get high praise? What is wrong with the focus of the answer in this paragraph?

How far do you agree that England's economy was transformed in the reign of Henry VII?

> England's economy was transformed to a large extent in the reign of Henry VII by the Navigation Acts. Under Henry VII, maritime trade was encouraged and developed. In 1493, Henry issued a trade embargo against the Netherlands because of its support for Perkin Warbeck. This led to a severe depression in the cloth industry. Prosperity only returned when the embargo ended in 1496.

Simple essay style

Below is a sample AS-level question. Use your own knowledge and the information on the opposite page to produce a plan for this question. Choose four general points, and provide three pieces of specific information to support each general point.

Once you have planned your essay, write the introduction and conclusion for the essay. The introduction should list the points to be discussed in the essay. The conclusion should summarise the key points and justify which point was the most important.

'The expansion of England's international trade in the reign of Henry VII made the most significant contribution to the establishment of the Tudor dynasty by 1509.'

Explain why you agree or disagree with this view.

Religion, humanism, arts and learning

Religion

Religion and religious belief played a central role in the lives of the vast majority of people.

The parish church was the focal point of village life, and its priest the most respected member of the community. Parish priests offered advice, guidance and community leadership, while monks provided charity, education and employment.

The majority of people were devout followers of the traditional practices and beliefs of the Church. They attended regularly and, as part of their routine of life, they followed the Church calendar, which marked the religious feasts, festivals and holy days. While the priest's main preoccupation was the teaching and preaching on matters of death and judgement, heaven and hell, the parishioner was more concerned with baptism, marriage and burial.

Although there was a steady growth in **anticlericalism** from the late fifteenth century, the only **heretical** idea to have acquired a significant following in England in the later middle ages was **Lollardy**. This laid stress on the reading of the Bible and urged the clergy to confine themselves to their **pastoral duties**. However, systematic persecution in the early fifteenth century had forced Lollardy underground, and there was no resurgence under Henry VII. By opposing anticlericalism, Henry gained a valuable ally in his quest to secure the Crown. The Church taught that it was a sin to oppose or rebel against Henry VII.

Humanism, arts and learning

The cultural developments that were taking place on the continent in a movement known as the **Renaissance** (the 'rebirth' of art, architecture and letters) came late to England. Mainly it took a literary form known as humanism, rather than the artistic form, which was more typical in Italy.

Humanism was the return to the study of the original classical texts and to the teaching of the humanities as the basis of civilised life. It made its first appearance in England in the middle of the fifteenth century. Because literacy was confined to the upper levels of society, its followers were restricted to the educated class. The celebrated humanist scholar **Desiderius Erasmus** visited England for the first time in 1499 and was impressed with the high standards of classical teaching being fostered by **John Colet**, Dean of St Paul's Cathedral and founder of St Paul's School. Henry VII patronised this 'new' learning and his support led to the development of a humanist circle in the reign of Henry VIII.

Perhaps the most significant event of this period was the arrival of the printing press, brought to England from Germany in 1476 by William Caxton. A steady stream of major English texts and translations from French and Latin emerged from the press. This led to the growth of a wider reading public, the beginnings of the standardisation of the English language and the circulation of the radical ideas of Erasmus, such as free will and religious toleration. Erasmus was a prolific writer who began his career by attacking corruption and superstition in the church. One of his most famous publications was entitled *On the Freedom of the Will* in which he criticised Luther and questioned the validity of his religious ideas. Henry VII also made use of the printing press to spread propaganda justifying his succession to the throne and denouncing the rule of Richard III.

Support or challenge? a

Below is a sample question which asks how far you agree with a specific statement. The table sets out a list of general statements that are relevant to the question. Using your own knowledge and the information on the opposite page, decide whether these statements support or challenge the statement in the question.

How far do you agree that the main reason Henry VII succeeded in establishing the dynasty was due to the effectiveness of propaganda?

	SUPPORT	CHALLENGE
The invention of the printing press and its arrival in England		
Henry VII suppressed Lollardy and anticlericalism		
The Church supported the Crown		
The influence of the Renaissance		
The development of a humanist circle at the royal court		
The spread of literacy		

Mind map

Use the information on the page opposite to add detail to the mind map below to show developments in religion, humanism, arts and learning.

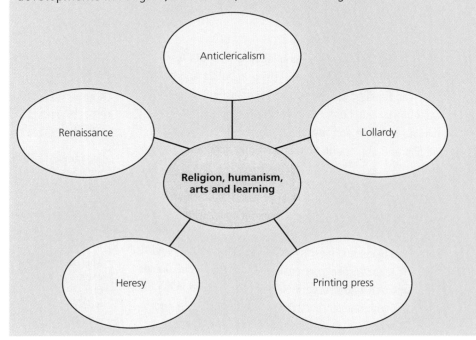

Exam focus

Below is a sample Level 5 AS-level essay. Read the essay and the comments around it.

'After 1485 Henry VII was so well established that he was never in any serious danger of losing the throne'. Explain why you agree or disagree with this view.

Henry Tudor's victory at Bosworth in 1485 did not necessarily secure him the Crown of England. The battle was but one of nearly a dozen fought during the Wars of the Roses, and although it was a stunning victory it did not guarantee Henry's safety after 1485. Henry had to work hard to secure his position and he remained vulnerable for many years after his coronation in October 1485. He was vulnerable because he was a usurper with a weak claim to the throne. Henry faced a number of dangers, chief among them were the Pretenders Lambert Simnel and Perkin Warbeck, who were supported by surviving Yorkists like John de la Pole, Earl of Lincoln, and Margaret, Duchess of Burgundy. This shows that Henry had enemies at home and abroad. However, Henry could not ignore the nobility either, because they had the power to depose him if he showed any weakness.

Henry had barely established himself on the throne before he faced serious challenges to his Crown. The first challenge came in the spring of 1486, when the Yorkists Lord Lovell and Humphrey Stafford attempted to raise a rebellion. The Lovell–Stafford rebellion failed due to a lack of support. A more serious challenge came in the summer of 1487, when a 10-year-old boy, Lambert Simnel, was used to impersonate the Earl of Warwick, a nephew of the dead King Richard III. This was a serious threat because Simnel was backed by John de la Pole, Earl of Lincoln and Margaret of Burgundy. The Simnel rebellion managed to gain support in Ireland and, with the financial help of Margaret of Burgundy, to raise an army of mainly mercenary soldiers. Although Lincoln was defeated and killed at the battle of Stoke, the fact that he had forced Henry VII to fight a battle showed how dangerous a threat the Simnel rebellion was. In battle anything could have happened; Henry might have been accidentally killed by a stray arrow!

This battle fatally weakened the Yorkist cause because so many leading Yorkists were killed. This made Henry stronger because he had won another victory in battle and had crushed and killed his Yorkist enemies. The nobility were so impressed by this victory that they were more reluctant to challenge Henry. This does not mean that Henry was free from danger. He still faced many enemies at home and abroad. Margaret of Burgundy was even more determined to depose him and she spent time and money supporting other pretenders, such as Perkin Warbeck.

Warbeck, like Simnel, was a young man who claimed to be a Yorkist prince, the younger son of Edward IV. He, too, first appeared in Ireland, but after the Simnel disaster few Irishmen were keen to join him. Warbeck posed a serious threat to Henry VII because he found support in Burgundy and Scotland. Margaret funded his plans and his travels to Ireland, Scotland and France seeking support. The French did not take Warbeck seriously, but the Scots did. James IV of Scotland thought he could use Warbeck in his quarrel with Henry VII. Scotland and England had long been enemies, and this was just one more attempt by the Scots to capture lands and towns in northern England, like Berwick. In the end, even James IV abandoned Warbeck, when he made peace with Henry VII and married his daughter. With Warbeck on the loose, Henry VII could not rest until the Pretender had been eliminated. This was a long time

This is a focused introduction that outlines the structure of the rest of the essay and states the overall judgement that Henry was not so well-established that there was no danger that he might lose the throne.

These are good opening and closing sentences as they make clear points which are focused on the question – 'established' and 'danger'.

This paragraph is well-developed, with a range of detailed examples relating to the danger posed by Lovell, Simnel, de la Pole and Margaret of Burgundy.

This paragraph provides context and offers an evaluation at an early stage in the answer.

This paragraph extends the range of the essay by introducing another key factor – Warbeck. There are also excellent examples, covering a good range of different aspects of the threats facing Henry VII from enemies abroad.

coming. Warbeck remained a potential threat to Henry VII for most of the 1490s. However, in 1495 Warbeck made a mistake when he invaded England with a small force. He was hoping to take advantage of the Cornish uprising against Henry VII, but he arrived too late. The Cornish rebels had already been crushed.

Even in prison Warbeck was dangerous because Yorkist supporters might try to free him. Warbeck was executed in 1499, when he persuaded his fellow prisoner, the Earl of Warwick, to escape the Tower of London. They failed and Warwick was executed. During this time, Henry was rocked by news that Sir William Stanley, the man who had helped him win the battle of Bosworth, was plotting against him. This plot was even more serious than either the Simnel or Warbeck rebellions because Stanley was a trusted member of the royal household. Stanley was executed in 1495.

> This paragraph concludes with one factor – Warbeck – closely followed by an appropriate reference to another – Stanley. This provides context with focused explanation. This clearly shows how the examples just mentioned answer the question, and comments on the dangers facing Henry VII, thus addressing why progress was slow.

Some historians claim that Henry was never really in any danger because, after Stoke, he developed an excellent intelligence system that warned him in advance of any plots or rebellions against him. Also, the Pretenders were clearly impostors and no one really believed they were who they claimed to be. For example, Simnel claimed to be Warwick, but Henry publicly displayed the real earl. Only with the benefit of hindsight can it be argued that Henry was never in any real danger, but to contemporaries these were very real threats.

> This is a good evaluative paragraph because it questions the premise of the question and attempts to offer a different interpretation.

It is fair to say that by 1499 Henry was well-established on the throne, and although he was not completely safe from plots to remove him, his deposition was looking highly unlikely. It was only in 1506 that he could feel completely safe, because Margaret of Burgundy had died in 1503 and the last of the Yorkist plotters, Edmund de la Pole, Duke of Suffolk, was captured and imprisoned. Therefore, I disagree with the view that Henry VII was so well-established that he was never in any serious danger of losing the throne after winning at Bosworth in 1485.

> This is a good conclusion because it summarises the key points of the essay and reaches a judgement based on reasoned arguments that disagree with the quotation.

This is a very good essay. The range of issues identified and corroborated in this answer demonstrates a very good level of appropriate knowledge. The premise of the question is addressed throughout, with some attempt to evaluate by exploring other reasons why Henry was not as well-established or free from the dangers suggested by the quotation. There is an attempt to reach a judgement. More could have been done to develop the potential threat posed by the nobility and to discuss the dangers posed by homegrown rebellions, such as the Cornish rebellion of 1497. No reference is made to the Yorkshire rebellion of 1489. Lapses in style should not be penalised too heavily, nor should lapses into narrative/description.

Reverse engineering

The best essays are based on careful plans. Read the essay and the comments and try to work out the plan on which this essay was based.

Exam focus

Below is a sample Level 5 A-level essay. Read the essay and the comments around it.

'Rebellions in the reign of Henry VII stemmed mainly from the weakness of central government.' Assess the validity of this view.

Henry Tudor's stunning victory at Bosworth in 1485 enabled him to claim the Crown of England, but it did not insulate him from the threat of rebellion. Henry remained vulnerable for many years because he was a usurper with a weak claim to the throne. Henry faced a number of dangers, and chief among them was the threat of rebellion. The causes of rebellion are varied: his political enemies, the Yorkists, wanted to remove him and replace him with a candidate of their own, but others, such as the commoners, simply wished to unburden themselves of crippling taxes. However, historians have broadened the debate by exploring other possible causes, such as the one proposed here – that is, weakness of central government. In order to assess the validity of this view, it is necessary to test the strength of the arguments for and against.

Arguments which support the view that rebellions in the reign of Henry VII stemmed mainly from the weakness of central government must, by necessity, include an examination of the role of the king, who was the head of the kingdom's administration. Henry had been in exile for half his life, so he was denied the opportunity to learn the mechanics of estate management, let alone the structures of central and local government. In short, Henry lacked the necessary experience to run a government. In an era of personal monarchy, where the king played a pivotal part in the exercise of power, it can be argued that Henry's lack of experience might have undermined the effectiveness of central government. For example, Henry tried, but failed, to win over some Yorkist nobles, such as the Earl of Lincoln, who was invited to participate in government. However, within 18 months of Henry's accession, Lincoln fled the government and led a rebellion that ended in disaster at the battle of Stoke. The fact that he so easily fooled his colleagues in government, and the government's failure to prepare properly for Lincoln's rebellion highlights its weakness.

Central government was dependent on local nobles and Justices of the Peace to carry out its orders. This dependency, by its very nature, must have weakened the king's government. In the early years of his reign, Henry, along with the men he appointed to run his government, was treated with suspicion. Some nobles, mainly Yorkist, did not trust him, or even wish to serve him, whilst others were weary of backing a king who might not last. If the nobility and JPs refused to co-operate, there was little the king could do. Central government might issue instructions, but they might not be carried out. It is important to note that central government had little understanding of local economic problems, although it was often blamed for them. Thus when Henry set about raising taxes to fund his wars against France and Scotland, the poorer regions, particularly the north of England, were unable and unwilling to pay. This lack of empathy and sympathy with the plight of the poor in the more remote parts of the kingdom underlines how weak the central government was.

The centralisation of government had yet to be firmly established, which meant that local and regional loyalties were stronger than national feelings. The people of Yorkshire and Cornwall rebelled, in large part, because they did not have an affinity, let alone a sense of loyalty to a London-based central government. They resented what they perceived to be interference in their affairs by an alien government. Their first loyalty was to their local community, and their second was to their region. The role of the local nobleman was crucial in fostering this sense of community, for the noble families often commanded a great deal of respect. If the noblemen

This is a focused introduction that outlines the structure of the rest of the essay, and provides a wider context to the debate by exploring other possible causes of rebellion in addition to the one proposed in the quotation.

These are good opening and closing sentences, as they make clear points that are focused on the question.

This paragraph is well developed with a range of detailed examples and provides context and offers an evaluation at an early stage in the answer.

This paragraph extends the range of the essay by introducing another key factor – local and regional loyalties being stronger than national feelings. There are also excellent examples, covering a good range of different aspects of the question, though it does tend to lapse into description.

Quick quizzes at www.hoddereducation.co.uk/myrevisionnotes

remained loyal to the king and followed the instructions of central government, then rebellion was far less likely to break out. The weakness of central government is most evident in the Yorkshire rebellion of 1489, when the king sent a former Yorkist, the Earl of Northumberland, to appeal to the rebels. As a northerner, it was hoped that his appeal for calm would quell the rebellion, but he was murdered because he was seen as an agent of an unpopular, southern, central government.

On the other hand, there are equally strong arguments against the view that the weakness of central government was mainly responsible for rebellion in Henry VII's reign. Some of the rebellions were clearly caused by economic discontent, which any weakness in the central government allowed, but did not motivate. The people of Cornwall and Yorkshire were simply too poor to pay the taxes demanded by the Crown, which is why they rebelled. They had no interest in removing the king or replacing his government. It can thus be argued that the weakness lay not in central, but in local government. For example, the Council of the North failed to heed the reports of popular discontent over rising prices and increasing unemployment. It was in a better position to understand the scale of local economic problems and to gauge the strength of local feelings.

The rebellions inspired by the Pretenders Lambert Simnel and Perkin Warbeck were politically motivated and would have occurred whether central government was weak or not. Their aim was to remove and replace the king and take over his government. Some of the rebels were motivated by personal ambition, such as Lovell and the Stafford brothers. It is important to note that the rebellions which took place while Henry VII was on the throne occurred in the first half of his reign. There were no rebellions after the Cornish rebellion of 1497.

It must also be borne in mind that the central government established by Henry VII at the beginning of his reign was still operating at its end. There was a continuity of personnel that contributed to its stability and longevity. The men Henry appointed to run his government were experienced professionals. Men like Sir Reginald Bray, Archbishop John Morton, Bishop Richard Fox and Sir John Heron had served in a number of administrations, so they knew how to govern.

In conclusion, it can be argued that although there is some evidence to suggest that the weakness of central government might have played a part in motivating rebellion, the other causes were far more important. Economic and political causes were far more significant causes of rebellion than the weakness of central government. Henry VII's central government may have been weak at the beginning of his reign, but as his rule progressed it became stronger and more confident.

This paragraph provides a very clear counter-argument by proposing another possible cause of rebellion – that is, economic discontent. It also directly challenges the premise of the question by suggesting that the weakness lay not in central, but in local government.

This is a good evaluative paragraph because it questions the premise of the question and attempts to offer a different interpretation.

This is a worthy paragraph that explores the strength rather than the weakness of central government, by highlighting the experience of the king's ministers.

This is a reasonably good conclusion because it summarises, if briefly, the key points of the essay and reaches a judgement based on reasoned arguments that disagree with the quotation.

This is a very good essay. The premise of the question is addressed throughout, with some attempt to evaluate by exploring possible causes of rebellion other than that suggested by the quotation. There is an attempt to reach a judgement. More could have been done to develop the counter-argument. The candidate adopts a straightforward for-and-against answer to the question, without attempting to offer a more integrated approach. More might have been said about the nobility and the role of regional councils.

Reverse engineering

The best essays are based on careful plans. Read the essay and the comments and try to work out the general points of the plan used to write the essay. Once you have done this, note down the specific examples used to support each general point.

2 Henry VIII and the Royal Supremacy, 1509–47

Henry VIII: character, aims and addressing Henry VII's legacy

Character and aims

Henry was not yet 18 (the legal age of majority was 21) when he succeeded his father as king in April 1509, but his minority did not require the appointment of a **regent** or lord protector. The contrast between the ill and aged Henry VII and his youthful and healthy successor could hardly have been more pronounced. This helps explain why many contemporary commentators regarded the change of monarch as the dawning of a new age. Henry's primary aims were to consolidate and extend his personal power and to ensure the succession and the continuation of the dynasty.

From the beginning of his reign, Henry was to demonstrate those qualities of decisiveness and ruthlessness that were to mark his kingship. This is not to suggest that Henry was infallible: he made mistakes, he occasionally vacillated, he could be cruel and vindictive, but he never lost his authority or his power to dominate people or events. It must be remembered that his chief ministers, Wolsey and Cromwell, were promoted and demoted by Henry, who did the same to their enemies, such as Thomas Howard, Duke of Norfolk, and **Stephen Gardiner**, Bishop of Winchester. This strongly suggests that Henry was the puppeteer rather than the puppet.

Henry was a man of strong convictions. He was convinced that, as king, he had a divine right to rule and that to question his judgement was akin to questioning God. He believed strongly that all that he did was done with God's approval. He was pious, but not deeply spiritual, being more practical and flexible in his religious beliefs. Henry was chivalrous and adhered to a strict code and concept of honour that remained unchanged throughout his life.

Addressing Henry VII's legacy

Henry inherited a stable, prosperous and peaceful kingdom. The dynasty was secure and the succession had passed without either incident or challenge. Henry's task was to build upon this solid foundation and honour his father's legacy. To address Henry VII's legacy, Henry VIII put in place measures to ensure the continuation of:

- strong and stable government, both at the centre and in the localities
- England's foreign policy, by honouring his pledge to marry Catherine of Aragon and thus maintain good relations with Spain
- the dynasty by marrying early in his reign, to improve the prospect of gaining a male heir.

On the other hand, Henry did depart from his father's legacy by ruthlessly disposing of his predecessor's chief financial agents, the unpopular **Sir Richard Empson** and **Edmund Dudley**, who were tried and executed for treason. Empson and Dudley were used as scapegoats for the most unpopular aspects of his late father's policies. Henry also abandoned his father's peace policy by pursuing rather than avoiding wars.

Delete as applicable **a**

Below are a sample question and a paragraph written in answer to this question. Read the paragraph and decide which of the possible options (in bold) is most appropriate. Delete the least appropriate options and complete the paragraph by justifying your selection.

How successful was Henry VIII in addressing his father's legacy?

> Henry VIII's attempt to build upon and honour his father's legacy was successful to a **great/fair/limited** extent. For example, he provided strong and stable government and he honoured his pledge to marry Catherine of Aragon and thus maintain good relations with Spain. However, Henry did depart from his father's legacy by ruthlessly disposing of his predecessor's chief financial agents, Sir Richard Empson and Edmund Dudley. He also abandoned his father's peace policy by pursuing rather than avoiding wars. Yet Henry VIII was able to govern England and pursue his continental ambitions from a position of strength.
>
> In this way, Henry's attempt to address his father's legacy was **extremely/moderately/ slightly** successful because

_____

_____

 How far do you agree?

Read Extract A about Henry VIII's character.

Summarise each of its arguments.

Use your knowledge to agree or contradict.

Arguments in extract	Knowledge that corroborates	Knowledge that contradicts
1		
2		
3		

EXTRACT A

He was a formidable, captivating man who wore regality with splendid conviction. But easily and unpredictably, his great charm could turn into anger and shouting. When he hit Thomas Cromwell round the head and swore at him, or addressed a lord chancellor (Thomas Wriothesley, Earl of Southampton) as 'my pig', his mood may have been amiable enough, but (Sir Thomas) More knew that the master who put his arm lovingly round his neck would have his head if it 'could win him a castle in France'. He was a highly strung and unstable hypochondriac and possessed of a strong streak of cruelty.

For all his power to dazzle, for all the charm and bonhomie which he could undoubtedly sometimes show, and for all the affection which he could certainly give and receive, it is difficult to think of any truly generous or selfless action performed by him, and difficult not to suppose that, even those who enjoyed his apparently secure esteem, like Jane Seymour or Thomas Cranmer, would not have been thrown aside if it had been expedient to do so.

Adapted from J.J. Scarisbrick, *Henry VIII* (Yale, 1997)

Government: Crown and parliament

Government

Henry VIII inherited a strong and stable central government, staffed by trusted advisers and efficient administrators. Regional councils and local government institutions were well-established. The Crown was solvent and the financial administration of the kingdom was tolerably efficient. Henry VIII also inherited some of his father's ministers, such as Sir John Heron, who continued in office until his death in 1521. The continuity in personnel strengthened the government.

The key feature of Henry VII's government was the king himself. His style of government was personal because he worked alongside his ministers, whom he consulted on matters of great importance. However, the final decision always rested with the king.

Unlike his father, Henry VIII was not prepared to work long hours and deal with the details of government business. He preferred to employ talented and energetic chief ministers whom he entrusted with the government and administration of the kingdom. As with his father, the final decision rested with Henry VIII, though he could be manipulated to adopt a different course of action.

Henry VIII's government was dominated by two exceptionally talented chief ministers: **Thomas Wolsey** and **Thomas Cromwell**.
- Wolsey was an effective administrator who attempted to make government more efficient. In 1526 he drew up the **Eltham Ordinances**, which attempted to professionalise the Crown's administration and reorganise the royal finances.
- Wolsey was succeeded by his former principal adviser, Thomas Cromwell. Cromwell has been credited by some historians with revolutionising the government. He aimed to bureaucratise the government by employing salaried civil servants, who adopted a more efficient and professional approach to the administration of the kingdom. The extent of these changes has been disputed by some historians.

Crown and parliament

The relationship between Crown and parliament can be described as that of a master and a servant. The king had the power to summon, **prorogue** and dismiss parliament. The traditional functions of parliament were threefold:
- Advice – to advise the king on matters of national importance
- Taxation – to raise revenue and supply the Crown with the money it needed to govern the kingdom
- Law-making – to draft and pass laws to ensure obedience and the maintenance of law and order.

Henry VII called parliament only seven times during his 24-year reign. Henry VIII made more use of parliament because he needed:
- money to pay for his expensive foreign wars
- laws to establish the Royal Supremacy.

During Henry VIII's 38-year reign, parliament was summoned nine times, but it sat for longer and dealt with a wider range of issues than those of his father's reign. The **Reformation Parliament** was summoned in 1529 and dismissed in 1536. It sat, though not continuously, for an unprecedented seven years, during which it was prorogued on seven separate occasions.

The 1530s are said to have marked a significant step in the evolution of parliament. It was used to effect changes in the constitutional relationship between Church and state. Henry VIII became head of the Church, with the power to effect changes in the state religion. Henceforth the financial and legal power of parliament grew in strength.

Turning assertion into argument

Below is a sample question and two sample conclusions. One of the conclusions achieves a high mark because it contains an argument (an assertion justified with a reason). The other achieves a lower mark because it contains only description (a detailed account) and assertion (a statement of fact or an opinion which is not supported by a reason). Identify which is which. The mark scheme on page 7 will help you.

To what extent was Henry VIII manipulated by his chief ministers Wolsey and Cromwell?

Answer 1

Overall, there is clearly some evidence to suggest that Henry VIII was manipulated by his chief ministers. Wolsey and Cromwell were professional bureaucrats who knew how the royal administration worked. The king relied on their advice and was persuaded by their arguments because he knew less about the day-to-day running of central government departments. Wolsey and Cromwell were able to take advantage of the king's reluctance to engage in the business of government and administration, which is why they were able to manipulate him. However, Henry retained the power of veto; he had the final say and there were times when he overruled his ministers. Clearly, there were times when Henry was manipulated into a particular course of action, but there were times when he controlled events.

Answer 2

In conclusion, the evidence suggests that the relationship between Henry VIII and his chief ministers was complex and did not conform to any set pattern. Henry could be dangerous and unpredictable, which made the work of his ministers altogether more difficult. There were times when Wolsey and Cromwell were able to manipulate the king by persuading him that he should heed their advice and follow a certain course of action. This is clearly seen when Cromwell convinced a reluctant king that contracting a marriage with Anne of Cleves was a good idea. Equally, there is sufficient evidence to suggest that Henry often 'allowed' himself to be manipulated because it suited his purpose. In the final analysis, it must be remembered that he had the final decision. No statute, injunction or proclamation could be passed or issued in his name without his knowledge or consent. Therefore, it is probably fair to say that Henry manipulated his ministers as much as they manipulated him.

Moving from assertion to argument

Below are a sample question and an assertion. Read the question and then add a justification to the assertion to turn it into an argument.

How far did Wolsey's and Cromwell's reforms lead to a significant change in some aspects of Henrician government in the period between 1515 and 1540?

There were some changes in Henrician government in the period between 1515 and 1540 because

_____

_____

_____

_____

Domestic policies, including securing the succession `REVISED`

Domestic policies

The primary focus of Henry's domestic policies was threefold:
- to extend the powers of the Crown
- to raise sufficient revenue to support his government
- to secure the succession.

Extending the powers of the Crown

Henry believed that the best way to maintain peace and promote law and order was by enhancing and extending the powers of the Crown. The authority of central government was strengthened and its power over the regional councils was extended. Royal commissioners were appointed to collect taxes, local law officers were selected to enforce the king's laws, and the powers of courts such as the **Star Chamber** were extended.

Cromwell's constitutional and government reforms in the 1530s, the so-called 'revolution in government', further enhanced the power of the Crown when Henry became the head of the Church. The unification of Church and state under Henry made him the most powerful monarch in English history.

Raising revenue

Raising the revenue necessary to fund Henry's policies proved more difficult than expected. Peacetime taxes were generally low, but wartime taxes tended to be very high. When Henry went to war with France (1512–13, 1522–25, 1544–46) and Scotland (1513, 1542, 1544–45), the need to increase the Crown's revenue became urgent.

As the Crown's financial demands increased, so did the opposition. Henry's tax commissioners took two years to collect the taxes levied in 1513. In 1523 the Crown demanded a subsidy of £800,000, but parliament was reluctant to grant it. The Crown's commissioners succeeded in collecting less than a quarter of the sum, around £150,000. The final straw came in 1525, with the **Amicable Grant**. This required the clergy to pay a tax of one-third of the value of their goods, while the rest of the king's subjects were expected to pay one-sixth. The fierce opposition to this tax shocked Henry. The king decided to abandon it rather than risk rebellion.

Later in the reign, Henry turned to exploiting the vast wealth of the monasteries to fund his domestic and foreign policies.

Securing the succession

Henry VIII's status and position as king was secure and was never in doubt. However, during the course of his reign he became concerned about the succession. His marriage to Catherine of Aragon had resulted in the birth of a healthy daughter, but not the longed-for son. Henry needed a male heir to succeeded him and continue the Tudor dynasty.

The king did not believe that a woman was capable of ruling England. The only example Henry had to draw on was that of Empress Matilda, whose claim to the throne in the twelfth century had led to bloody civil war. The Wars of the Roses were still fresh in the minds of an older generation, who feared a return to civil war should Henry be succeeded by his daughter, Princess Mary.

To secure the succession, Henry would need to annul his marriage to Catherine, to free him to marry someone who could bear him a son. From 1527 to 1537, securing the succession dominated Henry VIII's domestic policies. The birth of Prince Edward in 1537 settled the succession.

Spot the mistake a

Below are a sample AS-level question and a paragraph written in answer to this question. Why does this paragraph not get high praise? What is wrong with the focus of the answer in this paragraph?

'Royal government was transformed in the reign of Henry VIII.'

Explain why you agree or disagree with this view.

> Royal government was transformed to a large extent in the period 1509 to 1547 because of the administrative and financial reforms of the king's ministers. Royal government at the end of Henry VIII's reign was quite different from what he had inherited from his father. The Crown extended its power and raised more revenue, which shows that Henry and his ministers had been successful in transforming the government.

 Support or challenge? a

Below is a sample AS-level question which asks how far you agree with a specific statement. The table sets out a list of general statements that are relevant to the question. Using your own knowledge and the information on the opposite page, decide whether these statements support or challenge the statement in the question.

'The nature of royal government under Henry VIII was completely different from that under Henry VII.'

Explain why you agree or disagree with this view.

	SUPPORT	CHALLENGE
The Amicable Grant was an innovation in the assessment and collection of taxes		
Government became increasingly centralised under Henry VIII		
Henry VIII governed the kingdom through specially appointed chief ministers		
Henry VII was more successful in securing the succession		
Henry VIII was more successful in raising revenue		
Henry VII dominated the day-to-day running of royal government		
The unification of Church and state made Henry the most powerful monarch in English history		

Ministers: Wolsey, Cromwell, More and Cranmer

Ministers of the Crown

Monarchs had traditionally relied on a wide group of favourites to advise them and to carry out their orders. These favourites lived and worked at court, which is why the king's most trusted servants were handpicked from among this elite group of courtiers.

Henry VII relied on a small group of servants to advise him and work with him on the administrative detail of government. Henry VIII also relied on a group of favoured courtiers, but he singled out especially talented ministers, who were entrusted with greater royal authority to run his government.

Thomas Wolsey

Wolsey was perhaps the most powerful of those elite ministers who served Henry VIII. Wolsey owed to the Church his promotion and opportunity to serve the king. The Church was a meritocracy that enabled men of humble birth to rise to positions of power. Wolsey was a 'prince' of the Church: he was appointed Archbishop of York in 1514, made a Cardinal in 1515, and became a **papal legate** in 1518. Wolsey became the most powerful man in England, after the king, when he was appointed **Lord Chancellor** in 1515. This office effectively put him in charge of the government. His power was such that the majority of courtiers had to go through him to see the king. Wolsey served the king from c.1512 to 1529. He was dismissed after he failed to secure the annulment of Henry's marriage to Catherine of Aragon.

Thomas Cromwell

Cromwell, too, came from humble stock, but he opted for a career in the law rather than in the Church. His legal talent was spotted by Wolsey, who appointed him to his household. Henry VIII was also impressed by Cromwell's skill at finding solutions to difficult problems. Cromwell succeeded where Wolsey had failed by delivering the annulment and engineering the king's marriage to **Anne Boleyn**. Cromwell's administrative skill was held in high regard by Henry, who used him to run the government, manage parliament and establish the Royal Supremacy. Cromwell served the king from c.1532 to 1540, during which time he is considered by some historians to have revolutionised the government. He was dismissed from office and later executed because he was blamed for arranging and then failing to annul Henry's marriage with Anne of Cleves.

Thomas More

Thomas More was a lawyer, politician and humanist scholar. He was known and respected across Europe and was among the king's most favoured courtiers. More succeeded Wolsey as Lord Chancellor, but he served only two years (1530–32) before he resigned. More was a skilful and enlightened minister, but he could not support Henry's break with Rome or his marriage to Anne Boleyn. He was arrested and executed in 1535 for refusing to acknowledge Henry as head of the Church.

Thomas Cranmer

Cranmer was a theologian appointed Archbishop of Canterbury in 1532. Henry valued his honest advice and was impressed by the way he managed and enforced the Royal Supremacy. Cranmer was instrumental in reforming Church doctrine, supporting the publication of the Bible in English and embracing the Protestant faith.

Comparing interpretations

Compare the arguments in the two extracts and use your contextual knowledge to decide which is more convincing. You could shade the sections of each extract that you agree with.

Then set out the plan of an answer, identifying agreements between the two extracts and then disagreements, using your contextual knowledge.

> With reference to the two extracts and your understanding of the historical context, which extract do you find more convincing in relation to Cromwell's role in the reform of government? Give a reason for your choice.

Extract A argument(s)	Extract B argument(s)	Your contextual knowledge

EXTRACT A

When an administration relying on the household was replaced by one based exclusively on bureaucratic departments and officers of state, a revolution took place in government. The principle then adopted was not in turn discarded until the much greater administrative revolution of the nineteenth century, which not only destroyed survivals of the medieval system allowed to continue a meaningless existence for some 300 years, but also created an administration based on departments responsible to parliament – an administration in which the Crown for the first time ceased to hold the ultimate control. Medieval government was government by the king in person and through his immediate entourage. Early modern government was independent of the household, bureaucratically organised in national departments, but responsible to the Crown.

Adapted from G.R. Elton, *The Tudor Revolution in Government* (Cambridge University Press, 1953)

EXTRACT B

It has been argued over the last 30 years that Cromwell achieved a 'revolution in government' during the 1530s, though this interpretation has been attacked. The 'revolution' thesis maintains that Cromwell consciously – that is, as a matter of principle – reduced the role of the royal household in government and substituted instead 'national' bureaucratic administration within departments of state under the control of a fundamentally reorganised Privy Council. Such argument is, however, too schematic. The thesis that a Tudor 'revolution in government' took place is comprehensible when the periodisation of change is extended to Elizabeth's death, though whether the word 'revolution' is appropriate – as opposed to 'readjustment' or straightforward 'change' – is a matter of judgement. If 'revolution' is supposed to designate permanent change, it will not do.

Adapted from John Guy, *Tudor England* (Oxford University Press, 1988)

Mind map

Use the information on the page opposite to create a mind map to assess the contribution and impact each minister made in Henry VIII's reign. Read the question and complete the mind map with a sentence of explanation. Then rank them in order of importance.

> Which of Henry VIII's ministers made the greatest contribution and had the greatest impact in Henry VIII's reign?

The establishment of the Royal Supremacy

The king's Great Matter

Catherine of Aragon's failure to provide Henry VIII with a male heir weighed heavily on the king's mind. Henry chose to believe that because he had married his brother's widow, his marriage was cursed. He had fallen in love with Anne Boleyn, which convinced him to seek an annulment to his marriage. Anne was 15 years younger than Catherine and was more likely to provide Henry with an heir. The king's Great Matter came to dominate England's domestic and diplomatic agenda from 1527 until 1534.

Only the Pope had the power to annul the marriage, but **Clement VII** was reluctant to do so because of:

● Catherine of Aragon's spirited opposition – Catherine was advised and supported by respected scholars such as Bishop **John Fisher** of Rochester
● international pressure brought to bear by Catherine's nephew Charles V – as king of Spain and Holy Roman Emperor, Charles was the most powerful man in Europe; his decision to support his aunt and oppose the annulment, however, was due less to family loyalty and more to political and diplomatic reasons
● his predecessor's special dispensation to allow Henry and Catherine to marry – by granting the annulment, Pope Clement VII would have been questioning the validity of the dispensation issued by Julius II.

In the face of such strong opposition, Cardinal Wolsey unwisely promised Henry that he could persuade the Pope to issue a **papal bull** to annul the marriage. For his part, Pope Clement did all he could to slow Wolsey's progress.

After two years, the Pope finally agreed to hold a **legatine court** in England to judge the merits of Henry's case for annulment. **Cardinal Campeggio** was appointed to conduct the court at Blackfriars in 1529. The failure of the legatine court to come to a decision led to a stalemate and Wolsey's downfall.

The Royal Supremacy

For the next three years, pressure was brought to bear on the Pope.

Besides obtaining support from some influential European universities, Cranmer also drew up the ***Collectanea satis copiosa***, which made the theological case for the legality of the annulment.

The English clergy were browbeaten into submission. In 1531 they were charged with **praemunire** and forced to pay a huge fine of £100,000 to escape punishment. The **Supplication against the Ordinaries** (1532) accused bishops of abusing their power.

The king's Great Matter began to make substantial progress under Cromwell's leadership. In a series of laws passed through the Reformation Parliament between 1533 and 1534, Cromwell loosened the ties between England and Rome. The acts in Restraint of Annates and Restraint of Appeals broke Rome's financial and legal powers in England.

In 1534, the break with Rome was completed when the **Act of Supremacy** was passed. This denied the Pope's title and status, and instead recognised Henry VIII as Supreme Head of the Church in England. The establishment of the Royal Supremacy enabled Henry to govern the Church as he saw fit. It led to some changes in doctrine and to the dissolution of the monasteries.

Read Extract A and the two alternative answers to the question. Which answer focuses more on the content and which one focuses more on the arguments of the interpretation? Explain your choice.

With reference to this extract and your understanding of the historical context, assess how convincing the arguments in this extract are in relation to an analysis of Cromwell's merits as a chief minister in comparison with Wolsey.

Answer 1

This extract states that Cromwell was far more talented a chief minister than Wolsey. This is because Cromwell did not enjoy the advantages that came so easily to Wolsey. Cromwell was not as well-known in Europe as Wolsey, nor did he possess the experience of government that comes with age. Cromwell faced a tougher task in managing government because he had to contend with jealous courtiers and an inner ring of royal favourites. Therefore I agree with this argument because Cromwell was clearly a better minister than Wolsey.

Answer 2

This extract argues that Cromwell was a more talented minister than his old master Cardinal Wolsey. Cromwell merits this accolade because he had to overcome more obstacles than Wolsey, such as delivering the annulment and securing the Royal Supremacy. Unlike Wolsey, Cromwell was a not a 'prince' of the Church, so he had no high office with which to impress his contemporaries. Nor did he have the advantages of a European profile by means of his clerical offices which enabled him to exploit the Catholic's Church's continental contacts.

The extract convincingly argues that Cromwell had to rely on his legal and bureaucratic talents to impress the king. Cromwell proved to be a more efficient minister, being proactive in planning and securing the annulment that Wolsey had failed to deliver.

The extract also argues that Cromwell was in a different league to Wolsey because he had to deal with rivals in government and at court. That Cromwell is credited with being the architect of the Royal Supremacy in the 1530s is testimony to his talent and effectiveness.

EXTRACT A

Cromwell was not Wolsey in lay garb, and not merely because of his lower profile. First, the immediacy of the king's matrimonial problem and its knock-on effects on foreign policy and finance meant that Henry, willy-nilly, was much nearer to decisions on detail than he had been. Second, the 1530s required a minister who would be proactive and not reactive. Thirdly, Cromwell was in a different league to the Cardinal when it came to political originality. He needed to be. He did not have the advantages of age, European recognition and 'magnificence' which helped Wolsey to impress the king for so long. What is more, the greater involvement of the king meant that Cromwell had also to manage an inner ring whose members saw the king more regularly than he did. Nor did Cromwell escape inheriting the problem of the courtiers.

Adapted from by E. Ives, 'Henry VIII: the political perspective', in D. MacCulloch (ed.), *The Reign of Henry VIII: Politics, Policy and Piety* (Palgrave Macmillan, 1995)

Relationships with Scotland, France, Spain and other foreign powers

Henry VIII's relationship with foreign powers

Unlike his father, Henry VIII wished to play a more active part in international politics. Ignoring the dangers and the financial cost of potential conflict, he was keen to make England a major power in Europe. There were some notable diplomatic triumphs, such as the Treaty of London in 1518 and the **Field of the Cloth of Gold** in 1520. However, his continental ambitions had the potential to bankrupt and isolate an England that was among the less powerful and least wealthy nations in Europe.

Henry VIII was ambitious for power and glory. He believed that these could be obtained on the battlefield. His primary aim was to secure the French Crown, which he regarded to be his birthright. Henry drew inspiration from his hero Henry V, and the English victory at the battle of Agincourt in 1415. In pursuit of his aim, Henry forged alliances with some of the most powerful kingdoms in Europe, but he also made many enemies.

Scotland

Henry's relations with England's closest neighbour were often tense and unfriendly. The Scottish alliance with France marked out Scotland as a potential enemy. When Henry invaded France in 1513, James IV of Scotland took advantage of his absence to invade England. The Scots suffered a crushing defeat at the battle of Flodden, which also witnessed the death of king James. The succession of James V and the appointment of Henry VIII's sister, Queen Margaret, as regent for her infant son brought peace between England and Scotland. This peace lasted for nearly 30 years, until 1542, when Henry defeated the Scots at the battle of Solway Moss. War broke out again two years later, but it was short-lived.

France

Henry's claim to the French Crown inevitably led to conflict and put at risk the English possession of Calais. Henry invaded France three times, in 1512–13, 1522–25 and 1544–46. Although he enjoyed some victories, most notably at the battle of the Spurs in 1513, he also suffered defeats, such as the Gascony debacle in 1512, which resulted in stalemate. He never achieved his ambition, and the extent of his territorial gains amounted to the port of Boulogne.

England lacked the resources to conquer France alone. When Henry secured allies they tended to let him down. king Ferdinand of Spain failed to honour his promise to support the English in Gascony in 1512, whilst Charles V deserted Henry in his war with France in 1544 by making peace with the French king, Francis I.

Spain

At the beginning of his reign, Henry enjoyed a good relationship with his father-in-law, king Ferdinand. They became allies in war against France in 1512–13, but Ferdinand's lack of support for English forces led to military disaster in Gascony. Thereafter, relations between the monarchs cooled. The annulment of Henry's marriage to his Spanish wife made matters worse. The breach in the close relationship between England and Spain established with the Treaty of Medina del Campo in 1489 was never properly repaired during Henry's reign.

RAG – rate the timeline

a

Below are a sample question and a timeline. Read the question, study the timeline and, using three coloured pens, put a red, amber or green star next to the events to show:

- Red: events and policies that have no relevance to the question
- Amber: events and policies that have some significance to the question
- Green: events and policies that are directly relevant to the question.

> How far do you agree that Henry VIII's foreign policy was a triumph of ambition over substance?

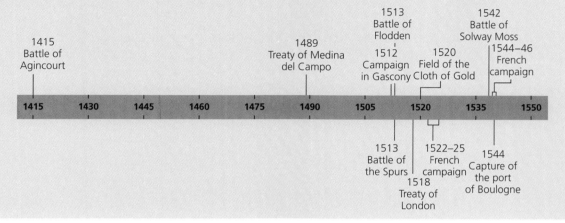

Introducing and concluding an argument

Look at the key points of the answer to the question below. How good is the proposed introduction and conclusion? Could either be improved?

> 'Henry VIII's foreign policy failed to achieve its aim of making England a major power in Europe.' Assess the validity of this statement.

Key points:

- Henry's more active and interventionist policy attracted the attention of the European powers.
- Henry's foreign policy consisted of peace and security at home, allied to war and annexation abroad.
- Treaties with foreign powers enhanced England's power and status in Europe.
- The scale of English military campaigns demonstrates Henry's commitment in European affairs.
- The readiness of European powers to forge alliances with England suggests that England was a major power in Europe.

Introduction

Henry VIII was ambitious for power and glory. His aim was to make England a major power in Europe, which is why he was determined early in his reign to play a more active part in international politics. There were some notable diplomatic triumphs, such as the Field of the Cloth of Gold in 1520, but there were also notable failures, like the Gascony campaign of 1512. In pursuit of his aim, Henry forged alliances with some of the most powerful kingdoms in Europe, but he also made many enemies.

Conclusion

In conclusion, there is no doubt that Henry succeeded in raising England's international profile, but he did not have the funds or resources to sustain an active and interventionist foreign policy.

Society: elites and commoners

Society in transition

The sixteenth century was a highly significant period because major changes were taking place within English society. Although the actual shape of the social structure had altered very little, mid-sixteenth century society was more competitive and individualistic than it had been during the Middle Ages. Even so, Tudor society was still overwhelmingly rural, and retained many of the characteristics of the old **feudal system**. One of the most important signs of change was the increasing social mobility between the various classes or social groups.

Elites

Due in large part to economic decline during the fifteenth century, many of the great aristocratic landowners had to sell part of their land and lease out much of the remainder on long leases of up to 99 years. The immediate impact of this was the temporary lowering of the social prestige of the nobility. They could no longer afford to maintain their great households, and service to the Crown became more attractive to the ambitious among the lesser elites or gentry. Likewise, the sale and leasing out of the great estates created a very active land market, which widened the availability of land. This redistribution of land marked the beginning of the rise of the gentry.

When prices and rents began to rise after 1500, due to improving industrial and commercial conditions, the gentry benefited from such increases. The aristocracy was unable to reap any real profit from their estates until the long leases ran out towards the end of the sixteenth century; only then were they able to repossess their land.

The rise of the urban elite

Henry VIII's reign also witnessed a rise in the status, wealth and power of the urban elite. These were the citizens and burgesses of large towns and cities, which included merchants, retailers and craftsmen who had made their wealth by trade. They were returned to parliament in ever-increasing numbers, which gave them a political voice.

Commoners

Significant changes were also taking place among the rural lower orders. The decline in economic and political power of the great landowners brought about the disappearance of **serfdom** and **labour services** in England during the fifteenth century. All the peasantry were now theoretically free (although there were still serfs in some parts of England until the end of the sixteenth century), so could move about the country more freely.

Changes in the structure of peasant society

This drastically altered the structure of peasant society. Peasant smallholders were generally described as husbandmen, self-sufficient smallholders with about 12–16 hectares of land. **Customary tenures** were being replaced by a new form of tenancy for the lifetime of the holder, called **copyhold**, for which rent was paid in cash. Many of the former peasants took advantage of the availability of land and amassed holdings of some 80 hectares or more. They became commercial farmers, and joined the ranks of the **yeomen**. Those commoners with skills and trades moved into the towns, where they were able to build up their businesses.

Support or challenge? **a**

Below is a sample AS-level question which asks how far you agree with a specific statement. The table sets out a list of general statements that are relevant to the question. Using your own knowledge and the information on the opposite page, decide whether these statements support or challenge the statement in the question.

'Tudor society in the reign of Henry VIII was a society in transition.' Explain why you agree or disagree with this view.

	SUPPORT	CHALLENGE
The social structure had altered very little		
The sale and leasing out of the great estates created a very active land market		
The urban elite enjoyed an unprecedented rise in their status, wealth and power		
Tudor society was still overwhelmingly rural, and retained many of the characteristics of the old feudal system		
The peasantry were now free and could move about the country more freely		
Merchants, retailers and craftsmen were returned to parliament in increasing numbers		
The redistribution of land marked the beginning of the rise of the gentry		

Simple essay style

Below is a sample A-level question. Use your own knowledge and the information on the opposite page to produce a plan for this question. Choose four general points, and provide three pieces of specific information to support each general point.

Once you have planned your essay, write the introduction and conclusion for the essay. The introduction should list the points to be discussed in the essay. The conclusion should summarise the key points and justify which point was the most important.

How accurate is it to say that the greater availability of land was the principal reason for the social and economic changes in Tudor society up to 1547?

Regional issues and the social impact of religious upheaval

Regional issues: Wales, Ireland and the north of England

The peripheral regions of the kingdom were remote, culturally different and economically poor. The Crown's power in these regions was tenuous at best, and the local populations tended to resent outside interference. The major problems affecting these regions were twofold:

- lawlessness and disorder
- a lack of respect for the authority of central government.

To remedy the situation, the Crown first appointed powerful nobles to represent and extend its authority. Although this system worked well under Henry VII, Henry VIII was determined to annex and bind these regions into a closer union with the rest of the kingdom.

Wales

Between 1536 and 1543, the government and administration of Wales was transformed by Cromwell's reforms. Lawlessness and disorder were the main problems facing the Crown in Wales. By virtue of the **Acts of Union**, Wales was fully integrated into the English state. The Welsh were forced to adopt English law, speech and customs. For the first time, Welsh members were elected to parliament, and Justices of the Peace were appointed to the newly created counties of the Principality.

Ireland

Unlike the peaceful assimilation of Wales, the Irish proved rather more difficult to control. English administrators were sent to govern the Irish – a task they accomplished with force rather than persuasion. The Irish parliament was closely controlled and an English army was stationed in the country. To demonstrate his power, in 1541 Henry VIII adopted the title of king of Ireland.

North of England

To govern this region, which to southerners seemed like a foreign country, the government set up the Council of the North, based in York. To the anger of northerners, southerners were often appointed to rule this region. The conservative north particularly resented Cromwell's instruction to close the monasteries. The monasteries were an integral part of northern life, which is why northerners rebelled in such large numbers in the Pilgrimage of Grace in 1536.

The social impact of religious upheaval: the dissolution of the monasteries

The most visible change in the Church and the nation's religion was marked by the dissolution of the monasteries, which were closed by Acts of Parliament. The 800 monastic institutions in England and Wales owned vast tracts of land, which they farmed at a profit. They also provided the population with a degree of social security, in the form of charity, hospitals and education. In many areas of the kingdom, their closure had a devastating impact on the social and economic well-being of the communities they served. The religious upheaval led to protest and rebellion in the north of England and in Ireland.

The Crown's attacks on the Church, and its propaganda portraying priests and monks as corrupt and greedy, added to the sense of despair felt by many parishioners. Religious reforms led to confusion and undermined the role of and respect for the parish priest. The Great Chain of Being came under greater scrutiny, as long-accepted social norms were debated and questioned.

Complete the paragraph

Below are a sample AS-level question and a paragraph written in answer to this question. The paragraph contains a point and specific examples, but lacks a concluding analytical link back to the question. Complete the paragraph, adding this link back to the question.

'In the period between the early 1520s and 1547, the dissolution of the monasteries had a significant impact on the lives of the people.' Explain why you agree or disagree with this view.

Following Cardinal Wolsey's dissolution of 29 monastic houses in the 1520s, over 800 monastic institutions in England and Wales were closed by the Crown between 1536 and 1540. The monks were forced to leave the monasteries, monastic land was seized by the Crown, and the buildings were largely destroyed by royal agents taking anything of value, such as glass, dressed stone and lead from the roof. The monasteries were important to the people in many areas of the kingdom because the monks provided charity, social security, education and medical support. In those areas where the monasteries played a pivotal part in the life of the community, their closure had a devastating impact on the social and economic well-being of the people. The religious upheaval led to protest and rebellion in the north of England and in Ireland. Overall, ...

 Developing an argument

Below are a sample A-level question, a list of key points to be made in the essay and a paragraph from the essay. Read the question, the plan and the sample paragraph. Rewrite the paragraph in order to develop an argument. Your paragraph should answer the question directly, and set out the evidence that supports your argument. Crucially, it should develop an argument by setting out a general answer to the question and reasons that support this.

'In the years between 1525 and 1547, the Crown was successful in extending its power into the regions.' Assess the validity of this view.

Key points:

- The passing of the Acts of Union
- Close control of the Irish Parliament
- The authority of the Council of the North
- Royal appointees given the power to govern the provinces
- The use of force and the agencies of law and order to gain control.

Sample paragraph:

The peripheral regions of the kingdom were remote, culturally different and economically poor. The Crown's power in these regions was tenuous at best, and the local populations tended to resent outside interference. To remedy the situation, the Crown first appointed powerful nobles to represent and extend its authority. Between 1536 and 1543, the Acts of Union ensured that the government and administration of Wales was fully integrated into the English state. For the first time, Justices of the Peace were appointed to Wales and the country was represented in parliament. Ireland, too, was annexed when Henry VIII adopted the title of King of Ireland in 1541. The Irish Parliament was closely controlled, as was the Council of the North, which governed the north of England.

Economic development: trade, exploration, prosperity and depression

Economic developments in the reign of Henry VIII

The sixteenth century was shaped as much by underlying changes in society and the economy as by the actions of the ruling monarchs. The rise in population and the onset of inflation had a profound effect on the lives of ordinary people. The increase in commerce and industry and the search for new markets and countries to trade with added to the sense of change. For some, these changes brought wealth and opportunity, but for others they made the difference between life and death.

Inflation

Prices and rents continued to rise steadily after 1500. By the 1530s, grain and meat prices had doubled since 1510. This was due in part to the poor harvests of the 1520s, but prices showed no sign of falling, even by the late 1520s after a run of good harvests.

Debasements of the coinage, which began in 1526, became very frequent in the 1540s, when Henry VIII was desperately trying to raise money to finance his wars against France and Scotland. By increasing the amount of money in circulation while devaluing the coinage, debasement caused very rapid inflation of prices.

At the same time, the Reformation contributed to this process. Gold and silver ornaments, seized from the monasteries, chantries and churches, were melted down and turned into coins, so adding to the volume of debased coinage in circulation.

Agriculture and industry

New techniques, crops and methods of field rotation were introduced. A number of new crops, such as clover and lucerne, were being grown to improve fodder for animal feed. Industrial crops such as saffron, woad and rapeseed were being grown to produce dyes and oils for textile manufacture. At the same time, improvements were made to the techniques of breeding cattle and sheep.

A vital part of this process of improvement was **enclosure**, because it enabled the growth of more efficient, medium-sized farms. Much of the common land was enclosed and brought under more intensive cultivation.

The agricultural sector was just about able to feed the population, except in bad harvest years. As the population began to rise, surplus labour became available to work in industry. This led to a migration of rural workers to the towns, which increased in size and importance. The metal and coal industries witnessed a rise in production and in the numbers of workers employed. However, cloth maintained its place as the most important industry in England.

Trade

English trade was dominated by the **Merchant Adventurers**, who owed their dominant position to the large loans that they gave to the Crown, in return for which they were granted privileges denied to other English merchants. The Merchant Adventurers established themselves at Antwerp in the Netherlands, which was a major centre for the dyeing and finishing of cloth. Henry VIII had little interest in exploration or finding new lands; his focus was fixed firmly on increasing trade at the expense of rivals such as the Hanseatic League.

Develop the detail

Below are a sample question and a paragraph written in answer to this question. The paragraph contains a limited amount of detail.

Annotate the paragraph to add additional detail to the answer.

To what extent did England's economy change in the reign of Henry VIII, 1509–47?

> The period between 1509 and 1547 was shaped as much by underlying changes in the economy as by the actions of Henry VIII. The rise in population and the onset of inflation had a profound effect on the lives of ordinary people. The increase in commerce and industry and the search for new markets and countries to trade with added to the sense of change. For some, these changes brought wealth and opportunity, but for others they made life more difficult. One of the key factors promoting economic development was the increase in international trade.

Eliminate irrelevance
a

Below are a sample question and a paragraph written in answer to this question. Read the paragraph and identify parts of the paragraph that are not directly relevant to the question. Draw a line through the information that is irrelevant and justify your deletions in the margin.

How accurate is it to say that the most significant economic development in the reign of Henry VIII was the rise in inflation?

> There is little doubt that the rapid rise in inflation during the reign of Henry VIII was one among a number of factors that had a significant impact on the lives of the people. Prices and rents continued to rise steadily after 1509, and by the 1530s grain and meat prices had doubled. This was due in part to the poor harvests of the 1520s, but even after a run of good harvests prices showed no sign of falling. Merchants and landowners were determined to increase their profits — hence the failure to reduce prices. Other equally important factors that contributed to the economic development of the kingdom included the debasement of the coinage and the introduction of new techniques, crops and methods of field rotation in the agricultural industry. These factors had a profound effect on the lives of the people.

Protest, opposition and rebellion

Protest

Protest had long been a means by which the commoners could vent their anger and frustration at changes they disliked or disagreed with. The majority of protests that occurred during Henry VIII's reign were local and usually focused on the availability and affordability of foodstuffs. Occasionally they might be directed against a particular magistrate or royal commissioner whom they found to be overbearing, cruel or corrupt. Protesters rarely directed their ire against the king, whom they trusted, but the same cannot be said of some of Henry VIII's ministers. Cromwell was a particular hate figure, whom the population at large tended to blame for the ills of the state, its government and reforms in the Church. Anne Boleyn, too, was disliked because she had replaced the popular Queen Catherine. Having his ministers to blame for unpopular policies suited the king.

Opposition

Opposition to price rises, inflation and unemployment often led to outbreaks of violence, but the localised nature of the protest never seriously threatened the king or his court. However, when members of the ruling elite joined together to resist or oppose government policies, it became a matter of grave concern. Unlike the commoners, the nobility and gentry tended to focus on political and religious issues.

Opposition in the 1530s

At court, factions formed around powerful figures such as Thomas Cromwell, **Thomas Howard**, Duke of Norfolk, Queen Catherine and Anne Boleyn. The so-called Aragonese faction supported Catherine by opposing the annulment and the attack on the Church. The Boleyn faction supported the annulment, the reform of the Church and was actively promoting Henry's marriage to Anne. Others, too, became involved in the faction fight, such as Bishop Fisher, who campaigned against the break with Rome, and Sir Thomas More, who refused to accept Henry VIII as head of the Church.

Although Norfolk and Cromwell lent their support to the Aragonese and Boleyn factions respectively, they were involved in their own contest for power at court. Besides personal ambition, the issue that most divided them was religion. Norfolk was a conservative Catholic who resisted changes in the Church, whereas Cromwell was a radical Protestant who promoted reform.

Rebellion

Armed rebellion was by far the most serious threat to the Crown. Henry faced such a threat in 1536–37, when a series of rebellions in the north of England came together called the **Pilgrimage of Grace**. This was a widespread popular revolt that first broke out in Lincolnshire before spreading to Yorkshire. Nearly 40,000 people joined the rebellion, which proved to be the largest and most serious in the sixteenth century. It was caused mainly by resentment over the changes in the Church, particularly the dissolution of the monasteries. The monasteries were held in high regard in the economically poor north, and the people blamed Cromwell for their closure. The fact that the rebellion attracted members of the nobility and gentry added to its seriousness. At the very least, the rebellion was a threat to the maintenance of law and order in the north.

Comparing interpretations

Compare the arguments in the two extracts, and use your contextual knowledge to decide which is more convincing. You could shade the sections of each extract that you agree with. Then set out the plan of an answer, identifying agreements between the two extracts, and then disagreements, using your contextual knowledge.

With reference to the following extracts and your understanding of the historical context, which do you find more convincing in relation to the causes of protest, opposition and rebellion in the reign of Henry VIII?

Extract A argument(s)	Extract B argument(s)	Your contextual knowledge

EXTRACT A

In a society in which lawlessness and violence were never far from the surface, rebellion was seen by many as the worst of evils. The State had no standing army, not even a proper police force, to deal with the rebels, so that any local movement could easily develop into a major threat. The Pilgrimage of Grace was in some ways the archetypal protest movement of the century. One typical feature was the importance of local rumour, in an age when communication between regions was weak. The Lincolnshire rebels, for instance, believed that their parish churches were about to be pulled down, like the monasteries. It was characteristic that few of the Pilgrims wanted to rebel against the king himself. They combined a conservative loyalty to the established order with a hatred of Henry's 'evil councillors'.

Adapted from Dan O'Sullivan and Roger Lockyer, *Tudor England 1485–1603* (Longman, 1993)

EXTRACT B

The dissolution was claimed by Aske to be the greatest cause of the rising. There had been poor harvests in 1535 and 1536. In addition, many other agricultural issues seem to have been motivated the rebels, including enclosures and rack-renting (raising of rents). In most areas, these issues were put on the back-boiler when the commons and gentry joined together. Opposition to the king's demands for taxes was a consistent theme in the rebels' articles. There was particular hostility to Cromwell's initiative of taxing in time of peace, introduced in the Subsidy Act 1534. There was also opposition to the Statute of Uses, which was effectively a feudal tax on aristocratic landed inheritances. The north saw itself as under attack from a greedy Crown regime.

Adapted from D. Rogerson, S. Ellsmore and D. Hudson, *The Early Tudors: England, 1485–1558* (John Murray, 2001)

Spectrum of importance a

Below are a sample A-level question and a list of general points which could be used to answer the question. Use your own knowledge and the information on the opposite page to reach a judgement about the importance of these general points to the question posed. Write numbers on the spectrum below to indicate their relative importance. Having done this, write a brief justification of your placement, explaining why some of these factors are more important than others.

How far was opposition to the Crown under Henry VIII motivated by the reforms of the Church?

1 Parliamentary legislation on taxation

2 Political conflict at court

3 The dissolution of the monasteries

4 The effects of price rises, inflation and unemployment

Least important ←——————————————————→ Most important

Religion: Renaissance ideas, reform of the Church, continuity and change by 1547

Religion

The Reformation had a significant impact on the religious lives, experiences, beliefs and loyalties of English parishioners. The certainties of old and the comfort of familiar and habitual religious rituals had been swept aside in a tide of reform. The men mostly responsible, Cromwell and Cranmer, were determined to effect lasting changes in the Church. They were Protestant sympathisers who had embraced the ideas of **Martin Luther**, the German reformer who had broken with the Roman Catholic Church.

The Act of Supremacy (1534) and the dissolution of the monasteries led to radical change that permanently altered the structure of the Church. The monastic vocation was dealt a fatal blow, whilst the secular Church underwent significant reform. The Ten Articles (1536), backed by the Bishops' Book (1537), was designed to establish religious conformity by forcing parishioners to accept changes such as the reduction of sacraments from seven to three (baptism, **penance** and the **Eucharist**) and the adoption the **Lutheran** idea of **justification by faith**. Another visible change was the wholesale destruction of religious relics and images in parish churches and the translation of the Bible into English.

Whereas Henry VIII accepted the destruction of the monasteries, he was reluctant to embrace the destruction of religious icons and other images or monuments, known as iconoclasm. Unlike Cromwell and Cranmer, the king remained a Catholic and an opponent of Protestantism. To Henry, Luther was as much an enemy as the Pope. The shift towards a more Protestant doctrine under Cromwell enabled the conservative faction led by the Duke of Norfolk and Stephen Gardiner, Bishop of Winchester, to persuade the king that the religious reforms had gone too far.

Henry responded by passing the Act of Six Articles (1539), which marked a return to Catholic doctrine. The sacraments were restored to seven and the doctrine of **consubstantiation** was replaced by **transubstantiation**. Following the fall of Cromwell in 1540, there were no more major changes, so that by 1547 the Church was a curious hybrid of Catholic and Protestant doctrine.

Renaissance ideas

The spread of Renaissance ideas, together with the rise of Christian humanism, were powerful influences that contributed to the Reformation and the weakening of the influence of the Church. Apart from causing a growth in anticlericalism by attacking the wealth and abuses in the Church, Renaissance thought encouraged the spread of secular education. Its emphasis on education for the laity helped to promote universities, the Inns of Court and secular schools as an alternative for political careerists. Previously, a clerical career was seen not just as an opportunity to obtain high office in the Church, but as a means of gaining important governmental positions.

Thomas Wolsey, who rose to become a cardinal, Archbishop of York and Lord Chancellor under Henry VIII, is seen as the last of the great English clerical careerists. His successors, such as Thomas Cromwell and **William Cecil**, came to power through a university and legal education. Increasingly, this became the route taken by those aspiring to a political and administrative career. The Renaissance, coupled with the break with Rome and the spread of Protestantism, contributed to breaking the political and economic power of the Church.

Summarise the arguments

Below are a sample question and an extract referred to in the question. You should read the extract and identify the interpretation offered. Look for the arguments of the passage.

With reference to the extract and your understanding of the historical context, how convincing do you find the extract in relation to the impact of the Reformation in England in the reign of Henry VIII?

Write down the interpretation offered by the extract.

_____

_____

EXTRACT A

Religious opinion in Tudor England was not to be created by Acts of Parliament. While the government swept away the connection with Rome and the monasteries, radical groups that were Protestant or nearly so, led by Thomas Cromwell and abetted by a half-Protestant Archbishop of Canterbury, were preparing advances on the liturgical front. The Ten Articles of 1536, the first of the Henrician formularies of the faith, reveal a degree of Lutheranism. The semi-official Bishops' Book of 1537 reflected Protestant influences. At the same time, two sets of ecclesiastical injunctions, of 1536 and 1538, began the reform of the new English Church.

Not even the conservative reaction of 1539–40, and afterwards, could halt the movement, despite the Six Articles Act, 1539, with its ferocious penalties. It is clear from Henry VIII's famous last speech of December 1545, with its impassioned plea for charity and concord, that the king was well aware that his experiment in Anglo-Catholicism might not survive his death.

Adapted from Denys Cook, *Sixteenth-Century England, 1450–1600* (Macmillan, 1980)

How far do you agree?

Read Extract B and summarise each of its arguments and use your knowledge to agree or contradict.

Arguments in extract	Knowledge that corroborates	Knowledge that contradicts
1		
2		
3		

Write down the interpretation offered by the extract and a counter-argument.

EXTRACT B

The literate elite in the age of Renaissance and Reformation has remained a vital area of study. What enhanced the significance of the Renaissance in Tudor England were the introduction of the printing press and the expansion of education beyond the clerical, academic elite to include a fair proportion of the nobility and gentry. The culture of the elite took on particular importance under the Tudors because of the Reformation. The leading writers of the age – humanists – had varying attitudes to the Reformation. The Tudor regime thought it vital that they should support the break with Rome, that their writings should legitimise the Royal Supremacy. The humanist schemes for education, which Wolsey had shared, were to be reshaped by the Reformation. The intellectual struggle involved in the Reformation put a high premium on the literary and scholarly skills of humanists.

Adapted from John Lotherington (ed.), *The Tudor Years* (Hodder, 1994 edn)

Exam focus

Below is a sample Level 4 answer on Interpretations. It was written in response to the following AS-style question:

> With reference to Extracts A and B, and your understanding of the historical context, which of these two extracts provides the more convincing interpretation of the effectiveness of Cromwell as the king's chief minister?

EXTRACT A

Once Cromwell identified the existence of a problem requiring a solution, he formulated it precisely (often, of course, with the aid of others), devised a solution which went to the root of the issue, converted this solution into practical politics by framing a specific measure of reform, and lastly endeavoured to apply it with tireless persistence. These are the familiar hallmarks of successful action, and one expects statesmen to possess such qualities. Few, however, in that age or in any other, have evinced them all consistently, and fewer still with the regularity of insight, speed of execution and relentless follow-through which distinguished Cromwell. Not without reason was he, who performed his promises, compared favourably with Wolsey, who was forever promising without hope or intention of performing.

Adapted from G.R. Elton, *Studies in Tudor and Stuart Politics and Government,* Vol. III (Cambridge University Press, 1983)

EXTRACT B

When Thomas Cromwell took office the secretary was essentially a member of the king's Household, whose importance lay in access to the king combined with an intimate knowledge of royal affairs, but whose status was not of the first rank. Because the secretary's role was not restricted to any particular area, Cromwell managed to exploit it to the utmost. He was able to extend his influence to virtually every area of public life and in so doing set a precedent that could be followed by later secretaries. He took the secretaryship out of the Household and made it one of the offices of state. Its new status was recognised in the 1539 Act of Precedence, where it was listed as one of the great offices of the realm. Cromwell supervised a change in governmental methods from Household practices to bureaucratic institutions.

Adapted from John Lotherington (ed.), *The Tudor Years* (Hodder, 1994 edn)

The extracts are useful in helping us to reach an understanding of Cromwell's role as the king's chief minister, but Extract B perhaps gives the most convincing interpretation because it refers to a concrete achievement by turning the secretaryship into one of the important offices of state.

This is a short but effective introduction that offers an opinion backed by a brief example.

The extract states that Cromwell not only saw the potential of the secretaryship, he 'managed to exploit it to the utmost' and 'was able to extend his influence to virtually every area of public life'. This helps to explain why Cromwell became one of the most powerful of Henry VIII's chief ministers. He was a skilled politician and a talented administrator, but he was also a man possessed of vision. Cromwell knew how the system of government worked because he had served his apprenticeship under Wolsey. This is supported by Extract A, which strongly suggests that Cromwell was a planner and visionary who 'compared favourably with Wolsey'.

This paragraph offers a reasoned discussion of the content of the extract whilst providing appropriate quoted passages. It also offers an explanation and refers back to the question.

Extract B is also convincing in its interpretation of Cromwell's effectiveness as a chief minister because it shows that he enjoyed the confidence of the king. Cromwell would not have been able to make the secretaryship into such an important office without the king's consent. His effectiveness as a royal chief minister is supported by the fact that he enshrined the change in an Act of Parliament. Cromwell was a very effective parliamentary manager. It was Cromwell's skill as a parliamentarian that first attracted Henry VIII's attention.

This paragraph is well-developed and offers a wider context by shedding some light on the relationship between the chief minister and the king, his employer.

The '1539 Act of Precedence' cemented the status and power of the office of king's secretary. These changes can be seen as part of a wider programme of governmental and administrative reforms which some historians claim amount to a 'revolution' in government. By taking the secretaryship out of the household and making it a bureaucratic office of state, Cromwell was professionalising the government. He is said to have done the same thing with the Privy Council, which came into existence during his period in office. The Privy Council may have originally been his idea because it was one of the suggested reforms of government listed in the Eltham Ordinance of 1526. Cromwell was Wolsey's chief adviser at the time.

This paragraph puts Cromwell's work as chief minister into context by showing that the changes referred to in the extract were part of a much larger reform programme.

Extract A is less convincing in its interpretation than Extract B only because it does not give any concrete examples of Cromwell's effectiveness as the king's chief minister. On the other hand, the extract should not be ignored because it was written by G.R. Elton, a distinguished historian. It was Elton who came up with the revolution in government idea, but in this extract he concentrates on Cromwell's personality rather than what he actually did. Some of what Elton says in Extract A can be used to suggest that Cromwell was an effective chief minister. For example, it describes Cromwell as a man of 'tireless persistence', who was adept at converting solutions 'into practical politics'. This suggests that Cromwell was not only efficient, but was a man of rare talent worthy of becoming the king's chief minister. The extract also states that Cromwell was a statesman, which fits the profile of an effective king's chief minister. What is important is the statement that Cromwell's effectiveness as a chief minister was not all down to him, that what he achieved he did 'with the aid of others'.

This paragraph extends the range of the answer by challenging the content of Extract A. It does well to note the attribution of the extract, though it could have done more to extend the discussion here.

Overall, it appears that Extract B is more accurate because it presents Cromwell more accurately than Extract A, which is a little vague.

This is a weak conclusion because it is too short, assertive and fails to offer a more rounded judgement supported by specific examples.

The answer is generally effective in approach, in that it seeks both to corroborate and challenge the arguments in each extract and reach a conclusion as to which is the more convincing, although the conclusion is assertive. It is more effective in its treatment of Extract B, where the knowledge cited is more relevant and appropriate. In its treatment of Extract A, it occasionally makes assertions from the written information. The answer could have been developed further in order to provide a clearer understanding of the overall arguments in each extract. This has the qualities of a high Level 4 overall.

Moving from Level 4 to Level 5

Read the comments. Make a list of the additional features required to push a Level 4 essay into Level 5. For example, the conclusion should be extended, less assertive and more factual.

Exam focus

Below is a sample Level 5 answer on Interpretations. It was written in response to an A-Level style question.

Using your understanding of the historical context, assess how convincing the arguments in Extracts A, B (see page 52) and C (see below) are in relation to Cromwell's role in the changes in government during Henry VIII's reign.

EXTRACT C

It has been argued over the last 30 years that Cromwell achieved a 'revolution in government' during the 1530s, though this interpretation has been attacked. The 'revolution' thesis maintains that Cromwell consciously – that is, as a matter of principle – reduced the role of the royal household in government and substituted instead 'national' bureaucratic administration within departments of state under the control of a fundamentally reorganised Privy Council. Such argument is, however, too schematic. The thesis that a Tudor 'revolution in government' took place is comprehensible when the periodisation of change is extended to Elizabeth's death, though whether the word 'revolution' is appropriate – as opposed to 'readjustment' or straightforward 'change' – is a matter of judgement. If 'revolution' is supposed to designate permanent change, it will not do.

Adapted from John Guy, *Tudor England* (Oxford University Press, 1988)

Two of the three extracts are more convincing in helping us to understand Cromwell's role in the changes in government during Henry VIII's reign. These are Extracts B and C, because they specifically refer to the changes in government and the part played in them by Cromwell. Extract A is less convincing because it is a personal description of Cromwell's character and talents as a politician and royal administrator.

Extract B argues that Cromwell was responsible for the changes in government because he 'supervised a change in governmental methods from Household practices to bureaucratic institutions'. To back this up, the author John Lotherington cites an example of Cromwell's changes. According to Lotherington, Cromwell made the post of king's secretary one of the chief offices of state. This reform transformed the structure of government because it effectively created a 'new' office at the heart of government. As king's secretary, Cromwell already had the power to control access to Henry VIII, but now he was able to control government. This change in the status, role and authority of the secretaryship had effectively created the office of chief minister.

On the other hand, the extract is limited because it does not discuss the wider changes in government. The reform of the secretaryship was not the most significant change in government, the 'creation' of the Privy Council is arguably the most important change, closely followed by the use made of parliament. The only reference to parliament occurs in Extract A, where Cromwell manages to get a bill through making legal the change in the status and authority of the secretaryship.

This is an effective introduction that offers an opinion backed by a brief explanation.

This paragraph offers a good discussion of the content of the extract, whilst providing appropriate quoted passages. It also offers an explanation and refers back to the question. It also offers some context to the changes in government mentioned in the extract.

This paragraph challenges the extract and provides some attempt to evaluate.

Although Extract A is rather vague, it does imply that changes in government did take place and that Cromwell had a part to play in them. It supports Extract B inasmuch as it states that Cromwell was a skilled politician and that if any changes did take place in Henry VIII's government, then he was the man with the talent and vision to carry them out. Cromwell was a man who found solutions to problems, and he was a man of his word by fulfilling his promises. The extract also mentions Wolsey, but does not expand on the close relationship between them. Cromwell had served Wolsey as his chief adviser, which role prepared him for the office of king's chief minister. Cromwell's service in Wolsey's household gave him an insight into the workings of royal government.

However, Extract C argues convincingly that Cromwell's role in the changes in government has been exaggerated. According to John Guy, the changes in government were not as significant as some historians have suggested. He is referring to Professor Elton, who argued back in the 1950s that the changes were so ground-breaking that they amounted to a revolution in government. Guy not only rejects the revolution in government idea, he also downplays Cromwell's role in the changes that did take place. Guy does not believe that 'Cromwell consciously – that is, as a matter of principle' reformed the government by setting up 'bureaucratic administration within departments of state under the control of a fundamentally reorganised Privy Council'. This is contradicted in part by what Elton says in Extract A about Cromwell being a 'statesman' and a political leader of 'insight, speed of execution and relentless follow-through'. However, in Extract A Elton does not use, refer to or even imply that a 'revolution' in government had taken place.

In conclusion, it is clear that, taken together, the three extracts do offer convincing arguments in relation to Cromwell's role in the changes in government during Henry VIII's reign. They all mention Cromwell and, to some degree, they do refer to his work as a politician and role in government. In addition, all three extracts make some reference to changes in government, either explicitly or implied. In my opinion, Extract C is the most convincing of all because it is written with some authority.

This paragraph attempts to compare two extracts and how one supports the other. It is rather vague on the content of Extract A.

This paragraph extends the range of the answer by offering an alternative interpretation to the other two. The author denies the scale of the changes and Cromwell's part in them. There is a valid reference and discussion of the author of Extract A.

The conclusion is valid and does attempt to round off the debate with a reasonable explanation.

This is a very good answer. The candidate engages with the question set and the arguments contained in the extracts are clearly identified. The candidate is clearly aware of the wider context and does attempt (not always successfully) to use this knowledge to corroborate and challenge the arguments in appropriate detail. The candidate attempts to offer a valid conclusion. This is a Level 5 response, but the limited challenge to Extract A places the response more to the middle of the level rather than the top.

Maintaining links

The sign of a strong Level 5 answer is the way it sustains an argument from start to finish, with each paragraph developing a key part of the argument. Examine the opening and closing paragraphs carefully and highlight where the candidate has presented and concluded their argument. In addition, give a heading to each paragraph to indicate which part of the argument is being developed.

3 Instability and consolidation: the 'mid-Tudor crisis', 1547–63

Edward VI: Somerset and Northumberland

Edward VI

Henry VIII was succeeded by the nine-year-old Prince Edward, his son by his third wife, Jane Seymour. Edward's succession was a problem because he was too young to rule, and periods of minority government were often times of potential challenge and political unrest. The fate of the 12-year-old Edward V must have weighed heavily on Henry VIII's mind. He had been entrusted into the care of his uncle, Richard, Duke of Gloucester, who was empowered to govern the kingdom as **Lord Protector**. His usurpation of the throne after just six weeks in the role provided a lesson for future generations.

Edward Seymour, Duke of Somerset

Henry VIII had tried to prevent trouble by establishing a Regency Council, led by Edward Seymour, Earl of Hertford. Seymour was Edward's uncle, which gave him a vested interest in the welfare of the young king. Henry had intended that Seymour should lead, but not dominate the Regency Council. Seymour was to govern with the aid of a council of ministers, specifically named by Henry VIII, who would share in the government of the kingdom.

However, Seymour was ambitious for personal power and he began to plot against his fellow councillors.
- By playing one councillor off against another, Seymour quickly split and then gained control of a divided Council.
- To underline his new status, the Lord Protector was promoted to Duke of Somerset by his nephew. The Lord Protector ruled the country for two years, until 1549.

During this time the political situation deteriorated steadily. This was caused in part by Somerset's arrogance and lack of ability. He was simply not up to the task of dealing with the numerous financial, economic and diplomatic difficulties which confronted the kingdom. Somerset's failure to deal effectively with the rebellions of 1549 was the final straw for his fellow councillors, who removed him in a palace coup.

John Dudley, Duke of Northumberland

From the ensuing power struggle, John Dudley, Earl of Warwick, emerged as the new leader. The 11-year-old Edward VI was in no position to oppose the change of leadership, even if he had wished to do so. Dudley was more energetic and capable a leader than Seymour. He put down the rebellions and restored law and order. He was promoted to Duke of Northumberland by the king, and he took the more consensual title of Lord President of the Council. The reference to the Council suggests that Northumberland was prepared to acknowledge and work with council members.

Northumberland ruled the country as Lord President for the remainder of Edward VI's reign. He was a talented politician who sought to unite rather than divide the Council. He adopted a far more pragmatic approach to government, and although he did achieve all his aims, he brought a measure of political and economic stability to the kingdom. He established a strong relationship with the young king, whom he encouraged to take an active interest in the business of government.

Spot the mistake

Below are a sample question and a paragraph written in answer to this question. Why does this paragraph not get high praise? What is wrong with the focus of the answer in this paragraph?

How far do you agree that the accession of Edward VI encouraged potential challenge and political unrest?

Henry VIII was succeeded by nine-year-old Prince Edward, his son by his third wife, Jane Seymour. A Regency Council was appointed to conduct business on his behalf. In this way, the story of Edward's reign tends to be about what the Council did, rather than the part the king himself played. Edward was a clever student who felt a great responsibility as heir to the throne.

Using knowledge to support or contradict

Below is an extract to read. You are asked to summarise the interpretation about Northumberland's abilities as a leader, and then develop a counter-argument.

Interpretation offered by the source:

_____

_____

_____

Use your knowledge to support this interpretation:

_____

_____

_____

_____

EXTRACT A

Politically the future lay with the Council, a Council whose members would in reality share the authority to govern England during the remainder of Edward's minority. It was Northumberland's genius to see that his political ambition depended on procedural control of such a Council. However, the fact that he achieved this control by February 1550 was the accidental result of the fiercest struggle for the powers of the Crown since the Wars of the Roses. In this struggle Northumberland simply aimed to avoid political destruction. Indeed, given the circumstances which he inherited in 1549, the duke of Northumberland appears to have been one of the most remarkably able governors of any European state during the sixteenth century.

> Adapted from D. Hoak, 'Rehabilitating the Duke of Northumberland: politics and political control, 1549–53', in R. Tittler and J. Loach (eds), _The Mid-Tudor Polity, 1540–1560_ (Macmillan, 1980)

Royal authority and problems of succession

Northumberland and royal authority

That Edward VI was a minor and of a sickly disposition in the last year of his life was a constant source of concern for Northumberland. Northumberland ruled in the king's name, so his position and power depended on the king's continued health and active support. This put Northumberland at a disadvantage, because critics could blame him rather than the king for the failings of government. Respect for royal authority tended to diminish when the king's government was conducted by ministers rather than the person of the monarch himself. Like Wolsey and Cromwell before him, Northumberland was portrayed as the 'evil councillor'.

Death of Edward VI

Edward VI's death in 1553 led a political and constitutional crisis. According to the terms of Henry VIII's will, Mary, the daughter of his first wife, Catherine of Aragon, was to succeed if Edward died childless. However, Mary was a devout Roman Catholic who hated the Protestant Northumberland. Northumberland feared that Mary would restore the authority of the Pope and so end the Royal Supremacy over the Church of England.

The device

In an effort to prevent this, Northumberland drew up the '**device**' and thereby tried to change the succession by disinheriting Mary and her younger sister Elizabeth, daughter of Henry VIII's second wife, Anne Boleyn. Instead, the Crown was to pass to Lady Jane Grey, the Protestant granddaughter of Henry VIII's sister Mary. Because of her royal connections, Jane became a victim of Tudor politics. Edward VI named Jane as his heir because of her attachment to the Protestant faith. The young king was determined to prevent his half-sister, Mary, from succeeding to the throne. In this he was helped by the Lord President, Northumberland, and by Jane's mother and father.

The accession of Queen Jane

To secure his own position, Northumberland planned to marry Lady Jane Grey to his youngest son, Guildford Dudley. Jane was persuaded to marry Northumberland's son and accept the crown after Edward VI's death. The plot seemed to have succeeded when the Privy Council initially agreed to proclaim Jane Queen of England.

However, when news of the failure of Northumberland's military expedition to defeat Mary reached the court, the majority of the **Privy Councillors** deserted Jane. They were soon joined by the majority of the ruling elites, both Catholic and Protestant, who rallied to the support of Mary. Whether they did this through dislike of Northumberland or to preserve the legitimate succession is not altogether clear. After nine days as queen, Jane, together with her husband and father-in-law, were imprisoned in the Tower of London. Northumberland was quickly executed, but Mary was reluctant to execute Jane because she accepted that the teenager was an innocent political pawn. However, when Jane's father led a rebellion against the Crown, Mary felt she had no choice but to execute her young cousin.

Complete the paragraph

Below are a sample question and a paragraph written in answer to this question.

The paragraph contains a point and specific examples, but lacks a concluding analytical link back to the question. Complete the paragraph, adding this link back to the question in the space provided.

To what extent did Edward VI's death in 1553 cause a political and constitutional crisis?

> There is little doubt that Edward VI's death was the primary cause of a political and constitutional crisis in 1553. According to Henry VIII's will, Princess Mary was to succeed if Edward died childless. In the event of her death, the Crown was to pass to Elizabeth. However, Mary was a devout Roman Catholic and Northumberland feared that she would restore the Pope and get rid of Northumberland. To prevent this, Northumberland tried to change the succession by disinheriting Mary and Elizabeth, and replacing them with Lady Jane Grey. Edward VI named Jane as his heir because of her attachment to the Protestant faith. Overall, …

_____

_____

How far do you agree?

Read Extract A in the yellow box.

Summarise each of the extract's arguments in relation to Edward VI's successor.

Use your knowledge to agree or contradict.

Arguments in extract	Knowledge that corroborates	Knowledge that contradicts
1		
2		
3		

EXTRACT A

The exclusion of Mary and Elizabeth from the throne and the setting up of Jane Grey to rule after Edward's death have been much debated. Whilst this would have made Northumberland the father-in-law of the Queen Regnant, Edward's 'Device' was not a plot hatched by John Dudley for his benefit. It originated with Edward to ensure a Protestant successor. It was only when he became really ill in the two months that Jane herself was made the heir. Undoubtedly, Northumberland would benefit, but when Jane had married his son, she was not the heir to the throne and it was expected that Edward would live long. Northumberland was merely making a wise marriage by connecting himself to his chief ally, the Duke of Suffolk. It was only later that this excellent marriage alliance was to give Northumberland's son a crown, however briefly.

Adapted from Matthew Christmas, 'Edward VI', in *History Review*, No. 27 (March 1997)

Edward VI and relations with foreign powers

Diplomatic inheritance

During the last five years of Henry's reign, his grasp on England's foreign policy was slipping. Peaceful diplomacy, it seems, had been abandoned in favour of military confrontation. The charge against Henry is that his final years were marked by war on two fronts – France and Scotland – in which he needlessly squandered his wealth and endangered the financial strength of his successors by attempting to win military glory.

Financial cost of war

In fact, the cost of the war was enormous, and by 1546 over £2 million mainly raised by the sale of monastic lands, had been spent, thus adding to the growing financial crisis enveloping the Crown. Henry's failure to achieve lasting success in France or to remove the ever-present threat of a Scottish invasion led to serious security problems for his successor. The simmering tension between England and her nearest neighbours only required a spark to ignite another conflict.

Foreign policy during the first part of Edward VI's reign was strongly influenced by the legacy left by Henry VIII – uneasy peace and costly defence. The young king's minority created fears over national security and the succession. There were major concerns over the possibility of renewed French intervention in Scotland and the end of the fragile peace.

Edward VI's foreign policy

The question facing Somerset was whether the war with France and Scotland begun by Henry VIII in 1542 should continue or not. Somerset inherited a war that Henry VIII had hoped would secure the marriage of Edward VI to the young Mary, Queen of Scots. Although the government was already bankrupt, Somerset continued the war and thereby further crippled the country's finances. At the same time, he strove to continue Henry VIII's policy of keeping on good terms with Charles V, ruler of Spain and the **Holy Roman Empire**, for fear of provoking him into war.

Growing demand for peace

Given the Franco-Scottish alliance, England's weakening military position in France and the chronic shortage of money, Somerset had done his best, but he knew that, in the long term, this was a war that could not be won. By the autumn of 1549, foreign affairs had reached a critical point. The war had become increasingly unpopular with both the nobility and the general public. High levels of taxation were undermining the economy and provoking hostility towards the government. For some time, Privy Councillors had been advocating peace as a means of restoring financial and economic stability.

Somerset's fall from power

Somerset's fall caused a temporary breakdown in military leadership. This enabled the French to gain the initiative in the war and they went on the offensive. Combined with a lack of money, this forced Somerset's successor, Northumberland, to make peace with both France and Scotland. This annoyed many of the ruling elites, who thought that this was a humiliating climbdown.

! Delete as applicable

a

Below are a sample question and a paragraph written in answer to this question. Read the paragraph and decide which of the possible options (in bold) is most appropriate. Delete the least appropriate options and complete the paragraph by justifying your selection.

How successful was Edward VI's foreign policy in the period 1547–50?

> Edward VI's foreign policy was successful to a **great/fair/limited** extent. For example, he continued Henry VIII's policy of keeping on good terms with Charles V, ruler of Spain and the Holy Roman Empire. In this way Edward's chief minister, Protector Somerset, was able to focus on France and Scotland without having to worry about Spain. On the other hand, Somerset realised that England lacked the resources, both monetary and military, to defeat the Franco-Scottish alliance. Nevertheless, Somerset's stubborn refusal to surrender to the Scots and French enabled Northumberland to bring them to the negotiating table and thereby pave the way for peace. In this way, Edward's foreign policy was **extremely/moderately/slightly** successful because

_____

_____

⧫ Mind map

Use the information on the opposite page to add detail to the spider diagram below to show how the different aspects explain English foreign policy between 1542 and 1550.

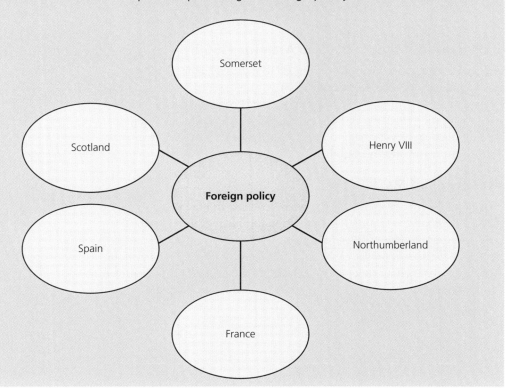

Intellectual developments, humanist and religious thought under Edward VI and Mary I

REVISED

The development of humanist and religious thought

The middle years of the sixteenth century were a pivotal period in the development of humanist and religious thought. The reigns of Edward VI and Mary I witnessed a fierce struggle between Catholics and Protestants, to win hearts and minds and, ultimately, for control of the state Church.

Beyond the parish and day-to-day experience of popular worship enjoyed by the majority of the people, the educated elites of both religious faiths – Catholics and Protestants – fought to win the cultural and intellectual battle.

- Inspired by the teachings of Erasmus, conservative humanist scholars, such as Bishop Stephen Gardiner, believed that a reformed Catholic Church could improve and enliven the religious experience of the people. He opposed the Protestants because he believed they were extremists and that their reforms went too far.
- Inspired by the teachings of **John Calvin** and Martin Luther, reformist humanist scholars, such as **Hugh Latimer**, believed that only a radical overhaul of the Church could transform the religious experience of the people. He opposed the Catholics because he believed the Pope and Church leadership were corrupt; they had let the people down and were incapable of reform.

The impact of the printing press

The humanist scholars of both sides were keen to spread their ideas. The printing press gave them the means to publish theological literature that would underpin the work of committed and charismatic preachers. Prime examples of the theological works being produced by Protestant authors during Edward VI's reign include:

- Cranmer's *Book of Homilies* (1547)
- Latimer's *Sermons of the Plough* (1548).

On the continent, the Catholic Church was also engaged in the production of theological tracts designed to keep pace with the increasing output of Protestant literature. This renaissance in Catholic humanist and religious thought became the foundation on which the Counter-Reformation was based.

Books of Common Prayer and the Forty-Two Articles (1553)

Protestant teachings and ideas adopted in Edward VI's reign led to radical changes. Cranmer's Books of Common Prayer and the **Forty-Two Articles** (1553), a list of essential doctrine, were intended to form the basis of the new Protestant Church of England. Protestant humanism also placed especial emphasis on educating the laity. Bishops were instructed to carry out visitations to encourage the adoption of the new services, and to test whether parishioners could recite the Lord's Prayer and the Ten Commandments in English.

Developments in the reign of Mary

During Mary's reign, many of Edward's religious changes were reversed and the Protestant ideas he promoted were rejected. As part of the Counter-Reformation in England, the Catholics followed the Protestants by promoting education and the printing of theological literature. For example, Roger Edgeworth's *Sermons very fruitfull* (1557), a collection of Catholic Reformation sermons, was designed to counter Protestant theology. The brevity of Mary's reign undermined a Catholic revival in England, and the succession of Elizabeth enabled Protestant humanist scholars to establish Protestant ideology and theology firmly in England.

Spot the mistake

Below are a sample question and a paragraph written in answer to this question. Why does this paragraph not get high praise? What is wrong with the focus of the answer in this paragraph?

How far do you agree that in the period between 1533 and 1558, Protestant humanist scholars were more successful than their Catholic counterparts in winning the hearts and minds of the English people?

The sixteenth century was a pivotal period in the development of humanist and religious thought. The reigns of Henry VIII, Edward VI and Mary I witnessed a fierce struggle between Catholics and Protestants to win the hearts and minds of the people of England and Wales. Humanist scholars of both sides were keen to spread their ideas. The printing press enabled them to publish theological literature which was used to underpin the work of hard-working preachers.

 Simple essay style

Below is a sample question. Use your own knowledge and the information on the opposite page to produce a plan for this question. Choose four general points, and provide three pieces of specific information to support each general point.

Once you have planned your essay, write the introduction and conclusion for the essay. The introduction should list the points to be discussed in the essay. The conclusion should summarise the key points and justify which point was the most important.

How accurate is it to say that the decades in the middle of the sixteenth century were a pivotal period in the development of humanist and religious thought?

The social impact of religious and economic changes under Edward VI: protest and rebellion

REVISED

The religious turmoil and economic difficulties that Henry VIII bequeathed to his successor put the new regime at a disadvantage. Edward VI's ministers, Somerset and Northumberland, could scarcely cope with the problems they faced, and their failure to resolve them led to two serious rebellions.

Religious problems

- Somerset inherited a divided Church that lacked decisive leadership and a clear direction. Somerset himself was a moderate reformer, as were most members of the Regency Council, whereas Edward VI favoured more radical changes. In 1549, Somerset sponsored Archbishop Cranmer's Protestant Prayer Book, which was intended for use in all church services.
- However, powerful pro-Catholic politicians, such as the Duke of Norfolk and Bishop Gardiner, were opposed to change, and such differences only increased the in-fighting among the political factions. Norfolk and Gardiner opposed the introduction of the Prayer Book, but its use was enforced by an Act of Uniformity.

To secure the support of Edward VI, Northumberland allowed increasingly radical reforms to be introduced into the Church of England. For example, altars were ordered to be removed, and the church service was modelled on the Lutheran and **Calvinist** systems of worship. In 1552, Cranmer introduced a second Prayer Book, which was far more radical than the first. This, too, was enforced by a second Act of Uniformity. Such moves not only angered the Catholic elites at home, but also antagonised Emperor Charles V, England's major continental ally, who was an active supporter of the Roman Catholic Church.

The social impact of the changes in religion was marked by confusion and anger. The population at large was largely conservative and resented changes in their local churches. The dissolution of the chantries in 1547 caused a lot of anger. This anger spilled over into armed insurrection in the Western or Prayer Book rebellion, which engulfed the south-west of England in 1549.

Economic problems

Somerset inherited an English economy that was in a very weak condition. Population levels had been increasing rapidly since the 1530s, causing prices to rise and making it difficult for young people to find work. The problem was made worse by a fall in demand for English textiles abroad, which caused growing unemployment among cloth workers. Changes to the pattern of landholding witnessed the wholesale enclosure of land, including common land. Pastoral farming was less labour-intensive than arable farming, which led to rising levels of unemployment.

Causes of the Kett rebellion

Rising inflation and increasing food prices added to the anger and frustration of the commoners. By 1549 there was widespread discontent, which led to a large-scale popular uprising in Norfolk in 1549. The Kett rebellion was largely caused by enclosure and resentment at greedy landlords, who were abusing their position of trust. Faith in the notion that those in society who had wealth and power should see to the social and economic welfare of those below them was breaking down. To the dismay of the uneducated laity, the principles of the Great Chain of Being were being debated and questioned.

Changes in government policy

The rebellions led to the overthrow of Somerset. Northumberland learned from Somerset's mistakes and introduced measures to try to restore social and economic stability. The Privy Council and the government were reorganised, finances were reformed and debts created by the war began to be paid off. Although the economic situation continued to worsen, a new poor law was introduced to help the poorest sections of society. The law created a new local officer in each parish – known as the collector of alms – who kept a register of all its licensed poor eligible for relief.

Spectrum of importance

Below are a sample question and a list of general points that could be used to answer the question. Use your own knowledge and the information on the opposite page to reach a judgement about the importance of these general points to the question posed. Write numbers on the spectrum below to indicate their relative importance. Having done this, write a brief justification of your placement, explaining why some of these factors are more important than others. The resulting diagram could form the basis of an essay plan.

To what extent was enclosure mainly responsible for the outbreak of rebellion in 1549?

1 Policy and impact of the enclosing of land

2 Division and political rivalry at court

3 Religious turmoil and economic difficulties inherited from Henry VIII

4 Decline and depression in the cloth trade

5 Radical Protestant religious reforms

6 Breakdown in the notion and principles of the Great Chain of Being

←——————————————————————————————→

Least important   Most important

 Simple essay style

Below is a sample A-level question. Use your own knowledge and the information on the opposite page to produce a plan for this question. Choose four general points, and provide three pieces of specific information to support each general point.

Once you have planned your essay, write the introduction and conclusion for the essay. The introduction should list the points to be discussed in the essay. The conclusion should summarise the key points and justify which point was the most important.

'The principal reason for the outbreak of protest and rebellion was the in-fighting among the political factions during the period between 1533 and 1558.' Assess the validity of this view.

Mary I and her ministers: royal authority and problems of succession

Mary I and her ministers

Queen Mary

Mary was the first ruling queen in English history, and in a male-dominated world she had to work hard at ensuring that her status and authority were respected. She began her reign well, displaying skill and resolution in defeating Northumberland's attempted *coup d'état*. This showed that she was determined to exercise her royal authority personally. Unlike her young brother Edward, she would not rule in name only, but would be fully involved in the business of government.

The Privy Council and councillors

The system of central and local government remained fundamentally unchanged during Mary's reign. The Privy Council continued to be the centre of the administration. One of the main criticisms of Mary's Privy Council has been that it was too large to conduct business effectively. In addition, it has been claimed that the Council contained some ministers of no real political ability and administrative experience.

The reason for this was that in the first few weeks of her reign, Mary was forced to choose councillors from her own Royal Household, and from among leading Catholic noblemen who had supported her. Within months, several moderate members of Northumberland's Council had been sworn in as councillors. Although this led to rivalry between the Catholics, led by Mary's chief minister, the Lord Chancellor, Bishop Gardiner, and the moderates, led by Sir William Paget, these ministers supplied a nucleus of political ability and administrative experience. However, it seems that Mary did not exert any leadership or show any real confidence in her Council.

The 'inner council'

Later in the reign, Mary tended to work with a smaller 'inner council' of experienced councillors, which included the Spanish ambassador, **Simon Renard**. As her reign progressed, she made less use of the Privy Council and only met with it when she had already decided matters of policy in consultation with Renard, who became her chief adviser. This angered her ministers, who were unhappy at being marginalised. By the end of her reign, Mary's relationship with her ministers had deteriorated.

Marriage and the succession

Mary's political inexperience and stubbornness can be seen in the first major issue of the reign – her marriage and the succession. The Privy Council was divided on the matter. There were two realistic candidates for Mary's hand:
- Edward Courtenay, Earl of Devon, who was favoured by Gardiner
- Philip of Spain, who was supported by Paget.

Courtenay was a descendant of earlier English kings and such a marriage would have strengthened the Tudor dynasty, but Mary favoured a closer link with the **Habsburgs** through Philip. Without consulting her Council, Mary announced that she was going to marry Philip, heir to the Habsburg Crown of the most powerful country in Europe.

The marriage treaty was very favourable to England. Philip was to have no regal power in England; no foreign appointments were to be made to the Privy Council; and England was not to be involved in or pay towards the cost of any of Philip's wars. If the marriage was childless, the succession was to pass to Elizabeth.

RAG – rate the interpretation   **a**

Read Extract A on Mary's character and personality.
- Shade the sections you agree with in green.
- Shade anything you disagree with in red.
- Shade anything you partly agree/disagree with in amber.

EXTRACT A

On the eve of her succession, Mary Tudor was in many ways old at 37, certainly embittered and otherwise fatally influenced by her peculiar apprenticeship. Not surprisingly, she would prove a distrustful queen. Having been rejected by or separated from those to whom she would normally have felt closest, she came to place her faith in ideals rather than in people. Chief among such ideals was her desire to marry, and perhaps to know as a wife and mother that domestic felicity of which she had been deprived in her own adolescence. Finally, and obviously linked to these other considerations, came her preference for and trust in Spaniards, who had ever been her aid and comfort, rather than Englishmen.

Adapted from R. Tittler, *The Reign of Mary I* (Longman, 1983 edn)

 Developing an argument

Below are a sample question, a list of key points to be made in the essay and a paragraph from the essay. Read the question, the plan and the sample paragraph. Rewrite the paragraph in order to develop an argument. Your paragraph should answer the question directly, and set out the evidence that supports your argument. Crucially, it should develop an argument by setting out a general answer to the question and reasons that support this.

> How accurate is it to say that Mary's obsession with Philip of Spain damaged her relationship with her ministers?

Key points:
- Marriage and the succession
- Division in the Council on the marriage question
- Mary's singlemindedness
- The influence of Simon Renard
- The development of an 'inner council' of trusted councillors

Sample paragraph:

Mary's relationship with her ministers was at its strongest at the very beginning of her reign. Mary's courage in refusing to yield to Northumberland impressed friend and foe alike. Mary seemed prepared to work with a wide cross-section of ministerial opinion, which engendered much goodwill. For example, within months of her accession, several moderate members of Northumberland's Council had been sworn in as councillors. Although this led to rivalry between the Catholics and the moderates, these ministers supplied a nucleus of political ability and administrative experience.

Mary I and relations with foreign powers

Mary has been condemned for being politically inept, for her obsession with Philip II of Spain and for her devotion to Catholicism. Mary has been criticised for indecision in the negotiations over the restoration of Catholicism to England and her marriage to Philip. However, recent research suggests that this was in fact masterly political inactivity and feigned weakness, designed to win greater concessions from the papacy and the Habsburgs.

The papacy

Mary had to be careful in her negotiations with the papacy. Her desire to restore the Pope as head of the restored Catholic Church in England worried those who feared an increase in foreign influence. To some, the Pope represented a foreign power and they feared that a restored papacy would demand the restoration of all Church lands and property confiscated during the reigns of Henry VIII and Edward VI. The fact that even staunchly Catholic landowners refused to give up former Church property forced the Pope to concede on this matter.

Spain and the Habsburgs

The fact that Mary was 37 years old when she became queen put marriage at the top of the political agenda. To secure the succession she must have an heir, but her choice of husband, Philip of Spain, put marriage firmly at the heart of England's foreign policy.

The Spanish marriage was as much diplomatic as it was personal, for the union of Mary and Philip also marked an alliance between England and Spain. The 1554 treaty with Spain revived an alliance first established in the Treaty of Medina del Campo in 1489. Mary had achieved her objective of forming a closer alliance with the Habsburgs.

The terms of the treaty stated that:
- the power to govern England rested with Mary alone
- England was not to become involved in or fund the cost of Spain's wars
- Philip was to assume the title 'king of England', but only for the lifetime of his wife
- if Mary were to die first, Philip would not inherit the English throne
- if the marriage were childless, the succession would pass to Elizabeth.

In spite of these safeguards Mary's popularity began to ebb because many people still thought that England would be drawn into Philip's wars and become a mere province of the Habsburg Empire.

Wyatt rebellion (1554)

Such was the strength of anti-Spanish feeling that it led to the Wyatt rebellion. The rebellion broke out less than a year after Mary's succession, and was led by men who had all held important offices at court under both Henry VIII and Edward VI. Although they had supported Mary's accession, they feared that the growing Spanish influence would endanger their own careers. The rebellion was crushed.

France

In spite of the terms of the treaty, England was drawn into Spain's war with France. In 1557, Mary declared war on France and an English army was sent to northern France to support its ally, Spain. The war led to the loss of Calais, England's last continental possession.

Eliminate irrelevance

Below are a sample A-level question and a paragraph written in answer to this question. Read the paragraph and identify parts of the paragraph that are not directly relevant to the question. Draw a line through the information that is irrelevant and justify your deletions in the margin.

'In the period between 1536 and 1558, the Crown's foreign policy was the principal cause of domestic unrest and rebellion.' Assess the validity of this view.

In some respects, it is fair to say that the Crown's foreign policy was responsible for the outbreak of serious unrest in England. For example, Henry VIII's break with Rome and his snubbing of Spain by annulling his marriage to the popular Catherine of Aragon led to a rebellion in the north of England. Later in the period, people feared that Mary I, as the first female ruling monarch, would be dominated by her Spanish husband and his male advisers. Her age was another factor. At 37, Mary was quite old for her first marriage, and it was feared that childbirth might result in her death. Childbirth was the biggest killer of women in the sixteenth century. The political elite feared another minority should Mary die and leave a baby as heir. The birth of a child would further endanger Elizabeth's life. As the focus of Protestant hopes for a return to the faith of her brother, Edward VI, Elizabeth posed a threat to Mary.

 Developing an argument

Below are a sample A-level question, a list of key points to be made in the essay and a paragraph from the essay. Read the question, the plan and the sample paragraph. Rewrite the paragraph in order to develop an argument. Your paragraph should answer the question directly, and set out the evidence that supports your argument. Crucially, it should develop an argument by setting out a general answer to the question and reasons that support this.

'English foreign policy largely failed to achieve its objectives in the years 1538 to 1558.' Assess the validity of this view.

Key points:

Arguments that may be used to support the premise of failure:
- Foreign policy in the 1540s was a costly failure
- Henry faced the threat of war on two fronts by 1544
- Failure of Somerset's foreign policy
- England became involved in Spain's wars
- Mary's failed campaign in France and the loss of Calais

Arguments that may be used to disagree with the premise of failure:
- Henry's success in negotiating a successful truce with France in 1546
- Mary's alliance with Spain, the strongest power in Europe
- Somerset's success at the battle of Pinkie and in stemming a Franco-Scottish invasion of England

Sample paragraph:

English foreign policy in the 1540s was both a financial and a military failure. Henry VIII failed to achieve his objectives, and by 1544 he faced the threat of war on two fronts. Somerset inherited a chaotic foreign policy and had to decide whether to make the French truce permanent or risk renewing hostilities. During Mary's reign, England allied herself with Spain and risked becoming involved in Spain's wars. Mary's failed campaign in France resulted in the loss of Calais. On the other hand, there were some successes, such as Henry's truce with France in 1546 and Somerset's success at the battle of Pinkie. Mary's alliance with Spain, the strongest power in Europe, should not be underestimated.

3 Instability and consolidation: the 'mid-Tudor crisis', 1547–63

The social impact of religious and economic changes under Mary I: protest and rebellion

REVISED ☐

By the end of her reign, Mary was unpopular. The problem was not the weakness of her character and policies, but her failure to produce an heir to consolidate her position. This, combined with the outbreak of war with France, religious persecution and the declining economic position, was the real cause of Mary's growing unpopularity.

Religious problems

Elizabethan propagandists were eager to depict Mary as a weak and unsuccessful, pro-Spanish monarch, in order to highlight the achievements of their own queen. Protestant reformers reviled her as a cruel tyrant, trying to enforce Catholicism through torture and burnings. Known as the Marian persecution, this has produced a popular picture of 'Bloody Mary' – a stubborn, arrogant, Catholic bigot, who burned some 300 Protestants and lost Calais to the French because of her infatuation with Philip of Spain.

In reality, Mary's proposal to return England to the Catholic faith was generally popular. However, when Mary's religious reforms became oppressive and turned to burning heretics, she lost support. The Protestant minority had always opposed her religious reforms.

Restoring the Pope

The Spanish marriage stoked up anti-Spanish feelings in a society already primed by Henrician propaganda to reject foreign influence. These issues led to the outbreak of the Wyatt rebellion, which aimed at Mary's removal and her replacement by Elizabeth. The rebels were also motivated by their Protestant beliefs and desire to undo Mary's pro-Catholic religious reforms. That they failed may be witnessed by the fact that a year after the rebellion, Mary felt confident enough to embrace foreign influence by restoring the Pope as head of the Church.

Economic problems

The Marian government inherited serious financial problems, which Northumberland had been trying to solve, such as **debasement of the coinage** and rising inflation. To make matters worse, Mary had given away Crown lands in order to re-establish some monastic foundations.

Consequently, during Mary's reign, the general economic situation grew worse, with a series of very bad harvests and epidemics of sweating sickness, bubonic plague and influenza. Towns were particularly badly hit, with high mortality rates and severe food shortages.

The government's reaction was to continue the policy, started under Henry VIII, of restricting the movement of textile and other industries from the towns to the countryside. This, it was hoped, would lessen urban unemployment and reduce the number of vagrants seeking work. This was short-sighted, however, because what was really needed was an increase in the number and variety of industries in both town and country, which would provide jobs for the growing number of unemployed.

The search for new overseas markets

To achieve this, the government needed to encourage the search for new overseas markets, to replace the trade lost with the decline of the Antwerp market. In 1551, English ships had begun to trade along the north African coast and between 1553 and 1554, Sir Hugh Willoughby was trying to find a north-east passage to the Far East. However, until 1558, successive English governments were too anxious to avoid offending Spain and Portugal to encourage overseas enterprise. It was not until the reign of Elizabeth I that any real progress was made in this direction.

Moving from assertion to argument

Below are a sample question and an assertion. Read the question and then add a justification to the assertion to turn it into an argument.

How far did Mary's religious reforms damage her image and reputation?

There is some evidence to suggest that Mary's image and reputation had been damaged by her religious reforms because

 Turning assertion into argument

Below are a series of definitions, a sample question and two sample conclusions. One of the conclusions achieves a high mark because it contains an argument. The other achieves a lower mark because it contains only description and assertion. Identify which is which. The mark scheme on page 7 will help you.

- **Description:** a detailed account
- **Assertion:** a statement of fact or an opinion which is not supported by a reason
- **Reason:** a statement which explains or justifies something
- **Argument:** an assertion justified with a reason

'Economic problems were mainly responsible for the outbreak of protest and rebellion in England in the period between 1536 and 1558.' Assess the validity of this view.

Conclusion 1

Overall, there is clearly some evidence that the serious economic problems affecting England during the 1540s and 1550s were responsible for protest and opposition to the Crown. The government was blamed for rising inflation and increasing levels of unemployment. It seemed as if the monarchy was unconcerned with the difficulties facing the people. The governments of the period were accused of neglect, being unable or unwilling to solve the economic crisis. In Henry's reign, Cromwell was blamed for the problems, as was Somerset during the reign of Edward VI. Mary's husband Philip and his Spanish advisers were also blamed for giving the queen bad advice. Mary seemed fixated on religious reform rather than solving the dire economic problems affecting the kingdom. War with France had only made matters worse. The people protested out of anger and frustration. The Crown had already faced a series of serious rebellions — the Pilgrimage of Grace and the Western, Kett and Wyatt rebellions — and it was feared that unless the economic problems were solved, others were likely to break out.

Conclusion 2

In conclusion, it can be argued that economic problems did contribute to the protest and unrest during the reigns of Edward VI and Mary, but it was only one of a number of factors. The economy had been in serious decline since the last years of Henry VIII's reign. Trade had been disrupted by war, which led to rising unemployment, especially in the cloth industry. Debasement of the coinage and inflation had led to rising food prices, which were always guaranteed to make the people restless. A hungry people are more inclined to protest because they are desperate and are, potentially, only a few days away from starvation and death. Government promises alone would not have been enough; action was needed. However, the Crown was distracted — for example, its preoccupation with religious reform and persecution — and the failing war with France simply added to the sense of crisis and neglect.

Elizabeth I: character, aims and the consolidation of power

REVISED

Elizabeth I

Character

Elizabeth, the daughter of Anne Boleyn, was 25 years old when she came to the throne. During Mary's reign, Elizabeth lived a precarious existence, partly because of her adherence to the Protestant faith, and partly on account of her position as heir to the throne. Unbeknown to Elizabeth, a group of prominent gentry laid plans to mount a rebellion against Mary, with the aim of establishing a Protestant regime, with Elizabeth as queen. The failure of the so-called Wyatt rebellion put Elizabeth's life in peril, for she was arrested and imprisoned in the Tower. Suspected of being party to the plot, Elizabeth was interrogated for two months and lived with the constant expectation of her death being announced. However, no evidence could be found against her and she was released and banished to an Oxfordshire manor, where she was placed under house arrest and kept under surveillance.

Aims

This experience had a profound effect on Elizabeth and shaped her personality and future conduct as queen. She became cautious to the point of being reluctant to take decisions, a fact that irritated and exasperated her ministers and closest advisers. The most important lesson she learned from her experience was her unshakable belief that she had been spared by God, who had chosen her to be his instrument on earth. This went a long way towards explaining the strong religious faith that she exhibited throughout her reign. Her primary aim was to establish a powerful position where she made the decisions. Elizabeth was determined not to be overruled by any man.

Consolidation of power

Given the political, religious and economic problems she had inherited from Mary, Elizabeth was well aware that the enthusiasm and popular support that accompanied her accession could evaporate overnight. She was determined to learn from the errors made by her predecessors, and in an effort not to repeat them, she quickly identified those issues that required careful attention: religion, finance, faction and the succession.

To consolidate her position, Elizabeth:
- put on a lavish spectacle to mark her coronation – this underlined her royal status as God's representative on earth, which reinforced her divine right to rule
- chose her ministers and advisers carefully – she appointed Sir William Cecil to be her chief minister, a shrewd move given Cecil's political and administrative experience
- summoned parliament within weeks of her accession, to settle the kingdom's religious and financial affairs.

! Summarise the arguments

Below are a sample question and the extract referred to in the question.

You should read the extract and identify the interpretation offered. Look for the arguments of the passage.

> With reference to the extract and your contextual knowledge, how convincing do you find the extract in relation to Elizabeth's character and personality?

Interpretation offered by the source:

_____

_____

_____

_____

EXTRACT A

At her accession Elizabeth's sex was looked on as a grievous disability, but she succeeded in turning even that to her advantage. Although she was sufficiently assertive to prevent her male advisers from contesting her authority, in other ways she flaunted her femininity, using it to appeal to the chivalrous instincts of the men who surrounded her, and inventing her dominion over them with an aura of idealism and romance. Furthermore, Elizabeth knew that, precisely because she was a woman, her ministers were ready to make allowances for her when she behaved in a fashion that would have been deemed intolerable for a king. Elizabeth exploited this indulgent attitude to stave off unwelcome decisions and to avoid being hustled into commitments against her will.

Adapted from Anne Somerset, _Elizabeth I_ (Weidenfeld and Nicolson, 1991)

! Develop the detail

Below are a sample question and a paragraph written in answer to this question. The paragraph contains a limited amount of detail.

Annotate the paragraph to add additional detail to the answer.

> How successful was Elizabeth's development of power as queen up to 1580?

Elizabeth ascended the throne in November 1558 to joyous acclamation. However, Elizabeth was well aware that the enthusiasm and popular support that accompanied her accession could evaporate overnight. She was determined to learn from the errors made by her predecessors, and in an effort not to repeat them, she quickly identified those issues that required careful attention. In one of her first acts as queen, she appointed trusted and experienced ministers to advise her and help her govern the kingdom.

Religious policy, the Elizabethan Church Settlement and relations with foreign powers

Religious policy

The question of whether the England inherited by Elizabeth was more Catholic than Protestant, or vice versa, is hotly debated. Indeed, the debate over the relative strengths of Protestantism and Catholicism is unlikely to be resolved because the issue is complex and the evidence contradictory. There were perhaps as many enthusiastic and committed Catholics as there were Protestants in England, but given the years of change and confusion, the majority of the people were possibly more inclined to be religiously indifferent. If the law compelled them to go to church, it was habit rather than conviction that impelled them to attend its services.

Elizabeth was Protestant and she intended that England would become a Protestant state. However, she did not wish to alienate her subjects, nor antagonise her continental neighbours. Thus Elizabeth's religious policy adopted an approach described as a 'via media', or middle way, between Catholics and Protestants.

The Religious Settlement

In such volatile circumstances, the majority of the population were ripe for conversion to either faith, which is why the settlement of religion was thrashed out in Elizabeth's first parliament. Meeting within eight weeks of her accession, between January and April 1559, parliament enacted the so-called **Elizabethan Church Settlement**.

The legislation re-confirmed the Royal Supremacy, set out the way in which the Church was to be run, and established the content and conduct of services in every parish church.

The Settlement included an **Act of Uniformity**, which established:
- a prayer book that was a compromise between the **Edwardian Prayer Books of 1549 and 1552**
- the **Thirty-Nine Articles**, published in 1563, revised from the Forty-Two Articles of 1553.

The government hoped that by being deliberately vague on some aspects of doctrine, the legislation would appeal to Protestants, without alienating Catholics. In short, the Settlement was a compromise capable of either a Catholic or a Protestant interpretation. Some Protestants were disappointed with the Settlement.

Relations with foreign powers

Elizabeth was keen to avoid war. Not only was war expensive, but it posed a very serious threat to her position as queen. Elizabeth was a lone female among a group of powerful male rulers. They might have regarded this as a weakness, but Elizabeth turned it into a strength. They might expect her to marry, so with that in mind they were more inclined to woo her than attack her.

Elizabeth's main concern was the reaction of these European monarchs to her Religious Settlement. Philip of Spain was prepared to give her the benefit of the doubt, in part because he hoped to persuade her to marry him. The French had religious problems of their own and were becoming preoccupied in civil war. In fact, one of Elizabeth's first acts as queen was to make peace with France, which was ratified in the Treaty of Cateau-Cambrésis in 1559. The Pope was also inclined to work with rather than against Elizabeth because he viewed the Settlement as a basis for discussion on the future direction of religion in England. Pope Pius IV believed he could persuade Elizabeth to embrace the Catholic faith.

Interpretations: content or argument?

Read Extract A and the two alternative answers to the question.

Which answer focuses more on the content and which one focuses more on the arguments of the interpretation? Explain your choice.

> Using your understanding of the historical context, assess how convincing the arguments in this extract are in relation to an analysis of the impact of the Religious Settlement during the reign of Elizabeth I.

Answer 1

This extract states that Elizabeth I's Protestant settlement of 1559 was responsible for reforming the Church of England. The rules of the Church were relaxed, which meant that parishioners could choose how they worshipped in Church: sitting, kneeling or standing up. Elizabeth had clear ideas on how she wished to reform the Church and was not prepared to be forced into changes she did not agree with.

Answer 2

This extract argues that the Church of England was reformed by Elizabeth and her government to a pre-prepared plan. The blueprint of the planned reform was contained in the Religious Settlement, which advocated a largely Protestant form of worship, backed by re-adopting the Edwardian Prayer Book. However, in an effort to avoid conflict between Protestants and Catholics, she insisted that the rules governing the new Church must be flexible enough to appeal to the majority of moderate parishioners from both sides of the religious divide. She rejected the Puritan demand to make the Church more Protestant because it might anger Catholics and push them into protest or even rebellion. In order to ensure the Settlement worked in the long term, Elizabeth passed the Act of Uniformity to provide an element of compulsion allied to consistency of worship.

EXTRACT A

Elizabeth's dominant place in British history is above all assured by the establishment and defence of the 1559 Protestant settlement – the English Prayer Book and Thirty-Nine Articles of Religion – which remains the basis of the Church of England today. Due to her determination, the Church of England remained sufficiently flexible and moderate. Elizabethan parishioners, for example, could take communion standing, sitting or kneeling, depending on the preferences of the community and its minister. Elizabeth would have no truck with those zealous Protestants who attempted to introduce the more austere [Puritan] discipline. In consequence, notwithstanding the strength of Catholic opinion at the outset of her reign, the Protestant form of worship imposed by her Act of Uniformity gained in popularity over time and became embedded in English culture.

Adapted from Susan Doran, 'Elizabeth I', *BBC History magazine*, Vol. 12, No. 8 (August, 2011)

Recommended reading

Below is a list of suggested further reading on this topic.

- Christopher Haigh, *Elizabeth I* (Longman, 1988)
- Susan Doran, *Queen Elizabeth I* (British Library, 2003)
- Judith Richards, *Elizabeth I* (Routledge, 2011)

Exam focus

Below is a sample Level 5 A-level essay. Read the essay and the comments around it.

'A mid-Tudor crisis is certainly an apt description of the period between 1540 and 1558.'

Assess the validity of this view.

Until recently, one of the most serious criticisms levelled at the Tudors is that they were responsible for a 'mid-Tudor crisis'. The monarchs most responsible for the crisis were Edward VI and Mary I. The reason why some historians labelled the period between 1540 and 1563 a crisis is because a strong king, Henry VIII, was succeeded by a boy-king, Edward VI, who in turn was succeeded by England's first female monarch, Mary. Edward and Mary ruled a kingdom that was plagued by financial, religious and economic problems. To make matters worse, the kingdom lacked good leadership; men like Somerset, Northumberland and Cardinal Pole did not know how to solve the problems. All this seems to add up to a crisis, but the idea of a 'mid-Tudor crisis' has been challenged.

> This is a focused introduction that outlines the structure of the rest of the essay, and states the overall judgement.

The idea of a 'mid-Tudor crisis' was supported by historians such as G. R. Elton, who said, 'After the rule of factions in the reign of a child, the succession of the wrong kind of Queen nearly completed the ruin of the dynasty and country'. Elton had a point, because Protector Somerset proved to be a weak and indecisive ruler who mismanaged the government. Financially, England was close to bankruptcy because of Henry VIII's debasement of the coinage and the massive increases in inflation. Somerset also inherited a war with France and Scotland from Henry VIII. The wars had seriously disrupted trade, which ruined the cloth industry, one of the biggest employers in England.

> Appropriate use of a quotation by a distinguished historian to debate the 'mid-Tudor crisis' label, followed by a critique of Somerset's rule.

Somerset's despotic rule caused some fellow councillors to plot against him. This caused factions to dominate politics at court and the king was too young to control them. Somerset's weak rule led to two serious rebellions – Kett's rebellion and the Western rebellion. These rebellions were motivated by economic grievances such as enclosure and religious grievances such as the Protestant Prayer Book. Somerset's faction rival, Northumberland, used the rebellions to take power. This would suggest that the crisis label is an apt one to describe Somerset's rule between 1547 and 1549.

> This paragraph is well-developed, with a detailed explanation of Somerset's failings as a ruler. Appropriate reference back to the question.

Northumberland was a more able ruler. He ended the wars, restored foreign trade, encouraged the cloth industry and ended the debasement of the coinage. To prevent future rebellions, he appointed Lord Lieutenants to watch over the shires. Northumberland adopted a more collective style of government, which reduced faction. Although he pressed ahead with making England a Protestant country, these changes did not cause a rebellion. Northumberland's government was quite successful, which does not support the quotation.

> This paragraph provides context and offers an evaluation of Northumberland's rule. It also challenges the question.

However, Northumberland did cause a crisis in 1553 when he tried to change the succession. This was a serious constitutional crisis because he tried to make Lady Jane Grey queen instead of Mary. Under the terms of Henry VIII's will, Mary was to succeed Edward, but Northumberland opposed this. He was supported by Edward VI, who knew that if Mary succeeded him, she would destroy Protestantism and restore Roman Catholicism to England. Northumberland realised that Mary would get rid of him. Northumberland's plan failed and the succession crisis passed quite quickly.

> This paragraph extends the range of the essay by applying the term 'crisis' to Northumberland's rule.

When Mary became queen, Northumberland was executed and replaced by her ministers, such as Bishop Gardiner and Cardinal Pole. They restored the Pope as head of the Church, persecuted Protestants and brought England into a closer union with Spain. Mary's religious and pro-Spanish policies were not popular with everyone. Some Protestant nobles, led by Sir Thomas Wyatt, rebelled. They were angry at Mary's intention to marry Philip of Spain. They feared Spanish influence at court and that England would be dragged into Spain's wars in Europe. Wyatt's rebellion was crushed and the marriage went ahead. Mary's obsession with religion made her very unpopular. The burning of Protestants caused discontent, and in 1557 England was dragged into Spain's war with France. The war was a disaster and England lost Calais. The war caused a financial crisis because it was expensive and England's lucrative trade with the Netherlands had been stopped. That Mary is remembered in history as 'Bloody Mary' suggests that her reign was a failure, so it can be argued that the term 'crisis' is an apt description.

> This paragraph deals comprehensively with the crises of Mary's reign. The question is referenced once again.

To conclude, it is difficult to decide if the term 'mid-Tudor crisis' is an apt description of the period between 1540 and 1558. Certainly there were moments of crisis, particularly during the rebellions of 1549 and 1554. It is important to note that in a reign spanning 38 years, Henry VIII only faced one rebellion – the Pilgrimage of Grace – whereas in the 11 years of Edward's and Mary's reigns, there were three rebellions. The financial, social and economic problems were also serious, but no more so than during Henry VIII's reign. One could argue that the financial crisis was caused by Henry VIII and inherited by Edward and Mary. In religious terms, too, there were serious problems, with the people being confused by the rapid changes between Protestantism and Catholicism. If there was a religious crisis in the reigns of Edward and Mary, then Henry VIII had one too. Therefore it is fair to say that we can find plenty of examples of crisis in the reigns of Edward and Mary, but we can also find them in the reigns of Henry VII, Henry VIII and Elizabeth.

> This is a reasonably good concluding paragraph because it shows an understanding of the problems in defining and applying the term 'mid-Tudor crisis'.

This is a good essay. The range of issues identified and corroborated in this answer demonstrates a good level of appropriate knowledge. The premise of the question is addressed throughout, with some attempt at evaluation. There is an attempt to reach a judgement. However the essay could be improved with some greater focus on the period between 1536 and 1540.

What makes a good answer?

List the characteristics of a good essay, using the example and comments above.

---

4 The triumph of Elizabeth, 1563–1603

Elizabethan government: court, ministers and parliament

Court, Privy Council and ministers

The most important element in central government was the Privy Council, and it was in its composition that Elizabeth achieved her first notable success. Elizabeth made it clear from the outset that she did not intend to repeat Mary's error in having a large Council, since it proved difficult to handle and often led to faction fights. The Council and Elizabeth's ministers were based at the court. The court lay at the heart of Tudor government because it was where the monarch lived, entertained and conducted the business of government.

Elizabeth expressed her intention to limit the number of councillors and she chose her closest advisers with care. Perhaps the most striking feature of her Council was the element of continuity, in that she retained some of Mary's councillors, while adding those of her own.

The two men most prominent in her government were:
- Sir William Cecil (Lord Burghley from 1571), who became her Principal Secretary of State
- **Robert Dudley** (Earl of Leicester from 1564).

Cecil's appointment added to this sense of continuity, since he had served in the government of Edward VI. The success of Elizabeth's Privy Council was put down to the fact that she introduced 'fresh energy and drive into the existing institutions'.

Parliament

Parliament had been and remained an occasional and peripheral part of the political system. There were only 13 sessions of parliament during more than 44 years of Elizabeth's reign, and no session lasted for more than a few months. The House of Lords was more powerful than the Commons, and it was to their lordships that government bills were first sent for debate.

It was expected that, in the Commons in particular, any questioning or querying of the queen's intentions would be moderate, cautious and highly respectful. Elizabeth drew a clear distinction between those topics which touched on her **royal prerogative** (and were therefore not to be discussed in parliament except by invitation) and those which had to do with the commonweal (which fell within parliament's competence). MPs generally were aware that religion, foreign policy, marriage and the succession were matters reserved for the queen and her closest advisers. However, this did not deter some radical members in the Commons, like Robert Bell, who organised a petition in 1566 to persuade Elizabeth to marry and settle the royal succession. It failed. Another area of dispute concerned free speech. Another radical MP, Peter Wentworth, believed that members of both the Lords and Commons should be entitled to speak freely on any matter. He was vigorously opposed by those MPs, mainly members of the Privy Council, who served the queen as parliamentary managers.

Elizabeth had to be persuaded by her ministers to call parliament. In 12 out of 13 parliamentary sessions, the argument used by her advisers was the need to arrange for the collection of taxation. When in session, parliament was invited to discuss a range of issues, such as religious reform, but debates and discussions were closely controlled by the Speaker. The monarch retained the final say on all matters by exercising the royal veto. That said, the relationship between Elizabeth and her parliaments was marked more by co-operation than conflict. Only when a bill received the royal assent could it become law. There is no evidence to suggest that Elizabeth deliberately obstructed parliamentary business.

Summarise the arguments

Below are a sample question and the extract referred to in the question.

You should read the extract and identify the interpretation offered. Look for the arguments of the passage.

> With reference to the extract and your contextual knowledge, how convincing do you find the extract in relation to the role of the Privy Council?

Interpretation offered by the source:

_____

_____

EXTRACT A

The Council under the Tudor monarchs actually ran the country. Elizabeth held membership down to a maximum of 19, and numbers tended to shrink as the reign went on. The Council's most important role was to advise the monarch on policy – although such advice was not included in the minutes recorded by the clerk, which are today our main source for its activities. What does appear in the minutes is evidence of the remarkable scope and variety of the Council's administrative work. Technically, it was not a law court, although it could carry out investigations, make decisions, and even commit offenders to prison.

Adapted from Dan O'Sullivan and Roger Lockyer,
Tudor England, 1485–1603 (Longman, 1993)

Simple essay style

Below is a sample question. Use your own knowledge and the information on the opposite page to produce a plan for this question. Choose four general points, and provide three pieces of specific information to support each general point.

Once you have planned your essay, write the introduction and conclusion for the essay. The introduction should list the points to be discussed in the essay. The conclusion should summarise the key points and justify which point was the most important.

> How accurate is it to say that parliament was the most important part of Elizabethan government?

Favourites and factional rivalries

Royal favourites

Elizabeth enjoyed the company of a number of royal favourites, the majority of whom were given high political office. They benefited from the queen's patronage and she delighted in their friendship.

Robert Dudley

The most significant favourite was Robert Dudley, Earl of Leicester. She and Dudley had known each other since childhood and they had both suffered together during the oppressive years of Mary's reign.

Dudley remained Elizabeth's favourite until his death in 1588. There had been strong rumours that they were lovers and that they intended to marry. They never did, but their close friendship endured occasional quarrels and jealousies, especially when Elizabeth entered into negotiations to marry a foreign prince. As a favoured courtier, Dudley also took an active part in government, becoming a prominent member of Elizabeth's Privy Council. This brought him into regular contact with Sir William Cecil, Lord Burghley, the queen's chief minister.

William Cecil

Cecil was another of Elizabeth's favourites, but their relationship was based on a close working relationship. He was an outstanding minister whom Elizabeth trusted to run her government. Elizabeth could be stubborn, but Cecil had the ability to persuade her to heed his advice and to act accordingly.

Other favourites

Other favourites who established a personal connection with Elizabeth included Sir Christopher Hatton, Robert Devereux, Earl of Essex and Sir Walter Raleigh. Raleigh was the only one who was never entrusted with high political office. Hatton was made Lord Chancellor, whilst Essex was Dudley's stepson, so he was especially favoured by the queen and was promoted to the Privy Council.

Factional rivalries

Dudley and Cecil became rivals in government, with both striving to outdo the other in terms of wielding influence. As high-ranking courtiers in receipt of royal patronage, they naturally attracted powerful supporters. Some of these supporters or clients were based at court, while others exercised their authority in the regions.

The Dudley and Cecil factions competed at court, though it must be said that before the 1590s they co-operated as much as they were in conflict. Faction fighting only really became serious from the 1590s, when a new, younger generation of courtiers took to the political stage. Essex was especially ambitious, and his determination to wield power by taking advantage of an aging queen's infatuation with him earned him bitter enemies. Among those opposed to Essex was Cecil's son and political successor, Sir Robert.

Essex rebellion

The Cecil–Essex rivalry reached its peak in 1601, when Essex rebelled. Essex's failure to defeat the Irish rebels, allied to his high-handed manner, proved too much for Elizabeth. Fed with a diet of unflattering stories about Essex's behaviour, Elizabeth turned on her favourite and banished him from court. Essex felt the only way to regain favour was to take control of the queen and eliminate Cecil. However, the rebellion failed and Essex was tried and executed.

Eliminate irrelevance a

Below are a sample question and a paragraph written in answer to this question. Read the paragraph and identify parts of the paragraph that are not directly relevant to the question. Draw a line through the information that is irrelevant and justify your deletions in the margin.

> How accurate is it to say that factional rivalry at court had been a serious problem throughout Elizabeth's reign?

Political competition, allied to personal ambition, lay at the heart of the factional rivalry that caused serious difficulties at court. The two most powerful members of the court were the queen's favourites, Robert Dudley, Earl of Leicester (from 1564), and William Cecil, Lord Burghley (from 1571). They became rivals in government, with each striving to outdo the other in terms of attracting the queen's attention. As high-ranking courtiers in receipt of royal patronage, they naturally attracted powerful supporters. Some of these supporters or clients were based at court, while others exercised their authority in the regions. Their disagreements over government policy often led to stalemate, with the result that some key decisions and some vital pieces of legislation were either delayed or abandoned. This struggle for dominance in the Council sometimes disrupted the smooth running of government.

RAG – rate the interpretation a

Read Extract A on the significance of royal favourites.
- Shade the sections you agree with in green.
- Shade anything you disagree with in red.
- Shade anything you partly agree/disagree with in amber.

EXTRACT A

The rebellion of the Earl of Essex is perhaps the clearest sign of a decline in Elizabeth herself. Until now, her favourites had been devoted to their queen. No one dared to rebel. Essex, although he was the poorest earl in England, was related to Elizabeth, for he was descended from her aunt, Mary Boleyn. More importantly, he was Leicester's stepson and had been brought up in Burghley's household. Such advantages gave Essex a head start over other courtiers, but it was his personality that secured his pre-eminence. Essex's relationship with Elizabeth was also stormy. In 1587, Essex accused Elizabeth of taking orders from Raleigh. Thus the story of Elizabeth and Essex was, from the beginning, one of quarrels, confrontations, rebukes and forgiveness. Essex did not perhaps fully understand the queen, underrating her experience and intellect, and did not appreciate that there were limits to the behaviour of even a royal favourite. The fact that Essex was also highly popular with the public did nothing to quell his ambition. Earlier favourites, including Leicester, had been unpopular, disliked because of their presumed ambition. Politically, Essex appeared to be playing a key role. Elizabeth had never allowed one man or faction to create rivalries that disrupted her court or council.

Adapted from Ian Dawson, *The Tudor Century* (Nelson, 1993 edn)

Foreign affairs: issues of succession, Mary, Queen of Scots and relations with Spain

REVISED

Marriage and the succession

As a woman in a male-dominated world, Elizabeth was expected to marry, and if she followed her sister's lead, her future husband was likely to be found among European royal families. Thus Elizabeth could benefit from the advice and security that marriage to a powerful European prince could offer. More importantly, the succession was at stake; therefore, in the opinion of her ministers, Elizabeth had to marry in order to provide the kingdom with an heir.

Elizabeth refused to bow to pressure and stated that she would not follow her sister's example and be dominated by a man, let alone a Catholic prince. She insisted that marriage and the issue of her successor were part of the royal prerogative and were matters for her alone. The problems Elizabeth faced were twofold:

- If she married a foreign prince in order to have a son, England might be dragged into the European power struggle.
- If she married a member of the English nobility, it might lead to envy, rivalry and the growth of dangerous factions.

Foreign affairs

Elizabeth used marriage as a tool in her foreign policy, holding out the prospect of marriage with foreign princes without ever committing to any of them. These princes included Philip of Spain, Eric of Sweden and Francis, the brother of the French king. This delicate balancing act proved effective until the mid to late 1570s when she passed the age of childbearing. By this time Elizabeth's relationship with Philip of Spain had broken down. Philip was encouraged by the Pope to make war on the heretic queen and invade England.

Mary, Queen of Scots

Unmarried, Elizabeth remained vulnerable, a fact made clear in the succession crisis of 1562, when she succumbed to smallpox. Without a named successor, her death might have plunged the nation into conflict, and it was only her recovery from the disease that averted the crisis. Her natural successor was her cousin Mary, Queen of Scots, but she was a devout Catholic. Mary's succession would not only imperil the Religious Settlement and the establishment of the Anglican Church, but would likely be opposed by the largely Protestant nobility.

The fact that Mary had been held captive in England since 1568 enabled plots against Elizabeth to be woven around the Scottish queen. In 1587, Elizabeth reluctantly agreed to the execution of Mary, after evidence was presented to her that revealed her cousin's involvement in the **Babington Plot**. With her death it was hoped the crisis surrounding Mary would be ended. However, it proved to be the excuse Philip of Spain needed to launch his Armada against England in 1588. The failure of the Armada finally put paid to the Mary, Queen of Scots affair.

Elizabeth opted to remain unmarried and reserved the right to nominate a successor. Only on her deathbed did Elizabeth finally name Mary's son, James VI of Scotland, as her heir.

Foreign policy 1580–1603

Elizabethan foreign policy in the period between 1580 and 1603 was dominated by Spain. English support for the Dutch rebels against Spanish rule in the Netherlands infuriated Philip of Spain. The escalating tension between the two nations was made worse by the success of the privateers in stealing Spanish bullion being shipped from the New World to the old. In 1585 tension turned to outright conflict with the beginning of the Anglo-Spanish War (1585–1604). This war lasted nearly twenty years and was only ended a year after Elizabeth's death in 1603.

Develop the detail

Below are a sample question and a paragraph written in answer to this question. The paragraph contains a limited amount of detail.

Annotate the paragraph to add additional detail to the answer.

How accurate is it to say that Mary, Queen of Scots posed a serious threat to Elizabeth?

In 1562, Elizabeth succumbed to smallpox and came close to death. This caused a succession crisis because she had no children to succeed her. Her nearest living relative with a claim to the throne was her cousin Mary, Queen of Scots. However, Mary was not a popular choice to succeed Elizabeth because she was a devout Catholic with strong ties to the French court. Mary's succession would imperil the Religious Settlement and lead to political division and conflict.

 Introducing and concluding an argument

Look at the key points of the answer.
- How good is the proposed introduction?
- How effective is the proposed conclusion?
- Could either be improved – especially in relation to Level 5 answers?

How accurate is it to say that plots against Elizabeth's life were a consistent feature of her reign after 1568?

Key points:
- There were at least five serious plots against Elizabeth's life between 1571 and 1586.
- The detention of Mary, Queen of Scots from 1568 until 1587 encouraged plotting against Elizabeth.
- The Pope's support of the plots against Elizabeth was a crucial factor.
- The execution of Mary in 1587 and the Spanish Armada in 1588 were also significant factors.

Introduction

There is some evidence to suggest that plots against Elizabeth I were a consistent feature of her reign after 1568. Five serious plots were hatched against Elizabeth between 1571 and 1586, and all were focused on her death and removal from the throne. The plotting reached its height in 1586, when Mary, Queen of Scots, finally agreed to support the Babington plot to murder Elizabeth. However, Mary's execution and the failure of the Spanish Armada marked the end of serious plotting against Elizabeth. So from 1588 until her death in 1603, Elizabeth was relatively safe.

Conclusion

In conclusion, there is little doubt that plotting against Elizabeth was taken seriously by the government and every effort was made to protect her. That Elizabeth died of natural causes is testimony to the success of those charged with keeping the queen safe from plots.

Society: wealth, social mobility, poverty and vagrancy

REVISED

Wealth and social mobility

Wealth creation and the increase in social mobility in Elizabethan England were more evident in the towns. The rise of the urban elite of burgesses, merchants and artisans was built on trade. As the wealth of this urban elite increased, so did their power. They monopolised municipal office, controlled parliamentary elections and generally governed the towns, largely independent of royal or noble control.

Apart from gaining a political voice in Elizabethan parliaments, they also invested their wealth in rural estates. In this way, burgesses became country squires and joined the landowning elite. Social mobility gradually turned into social integration, through marriage between the old landed elite and their new neighbours, the former townsmen.

Poverty and vagrancy

The plight of the poor was an ever-present problem that successive Tudor governments had been unable, and at times apparently unwilling, to solve. As the population increased, so did the pressure on land, food production and prices. Poverty increased in line with the population because of the pressure to provide work. Around 60 per cent of the population lived at or below the poverty line.

Even those in work faced difficulties, because the rise in wages failed to keep pace with the sharp increase in food prices. The landless poor were hardest hit because they no longer had the monasteries to care for them. Hungry, poverty-stricken, able-bodied peasants became vagrants, mainly because they were searching for work. Whilst some turned to crime to feed their families, the majority were law-abiding.

The maintenance of public order

The maintenance of public order was and always had been the prime responsibility of Tudor government. Tudor administrators feared disorder and protest because they might lead to rebellion. The fear of vagrants, or 'masterless men', was uppermost in the minds of Tudor legislators because they had no control over these mobile groups of wanderers. Their independence undermined the ideas set out in the Great Chain of Being. The link between unemployment and crime was not universally accepted, but the notion that men without masters were likely committing crime was. The Edwardian Vagrancy Act of 1547 set a new level of barbarity in the cruel treatment of the vagrant poor. Punishment, rather than relief, was the order of the day.

Relief rather than repression

This attitude had changed somewhat during Elizabeth's reign, when it became apparent that punishment alone was unlikely to solve poverty and vagrancy. The Statute of Artificers (1563) was a legislative achievement because it encouraged apprenticeships for men and directed women into domestic service. The drive to understand and improve the plight of the poor and vagrant culminated in the more enlightened Acts of 1598 and 1601, which set up a system of poor relief across the kingdom. The Church encouraged charity and philanthropy. The most generous benefactors to the poor were the merchants and fellow townsmen, who helped fund hospitals and schools. The passing of the Poor Laws during the sixteenth century had encouraged a significant change in attitude to the poor and vagrants. By highlighting the plight of the poor, allied to a greater understanding of the causes of poverty, the rich were more inclined to relieve than suppress their less fortunate fellow citizens.

Support or challenge?   a

Below is a sample question which asks how far you agree with a specific statement.
The table sets out a list of general statements that are relevant to the question. Using
your own knowledge and the information on the opposite page, decide whether these
statements support or challenge the statement in the question.

How far do you agree that vagrancy was a threat to the Elizabethan state?

	SUPPORT	CHALLENGE
The maintenance of public order was the prime responsibility of Tudor government		
The landed elite feared disorder and protest because they might lead to rebellion		
There was widespread belief that men without masters were inclined to commit crime		
The wealth of the urban elite had increased substantially		
Sixty per cent of the population lived at or below the poverty line		
Social mobility gradually turned into social integration through marriage		

Spectrum of importance   a

Below are a sample question and a list of general points that could be used to answer
the question. Use your own knowledge and the information on the opposite page
to reach a judgement about the importance of these general points to the question
posed. Write numbers on the spectrum below to indicate their relative importance.
Having done this, write a brief justification of your placement, explaining why some of
these factors are more important than others. The resulting diagram could form the
basis of an essay plan.

To what extent had attitudes to the poor and vagrant changed by the end
of Elizabeth's reign?

1 The Edwardian Vagrancy Act, 1547

2 The Statute of Artificers, 1563

3 Fear of widespread crime, disorder and protest

4 The role of the Church

5 Parliamentary Acts of 1598 and 1601 and the setting up of a system of poor relief

6 Breakdown in the notion and principles of the Great Chain of Being

Least important   Most important

Problems in the regions, social discontent and rebellions

REVISED

The issues that most divided the people of England were religion and the economy. The division between Catholic and Protestant was brought into sharper relief when the Religious Settlement collapsed in 1570. Elizabeth's **excommunication** by the Pope led to the enactment of laws against Catholics. Persecuted and penalised, the more committed among them, known as **recusants**, were willing to contemplate plots and rebellion.

The Northern rebellion, 1569–70

The more religiously conservative and economically disadvantaged north of England witnessed one of the most serious rebellions of Elizabeth's reign. The Northern rebellion (also known as the rebellion of the Northern Earls), led by the Earls of Northumberland and Westmorland, was motivated by political and religious frustrations. The earls resented being marginalised at court and had never truly accepted the Protestant Religious Settlement. The detention of Mary, Queen of Scots, acted as a catalyst for rebellion. The rebellion failed because the majority of the people of the northern counties were disinclined to support it. It was a noble rebellion, supported in the main by the leaders' tenants. The people of the north were more concerned about the availability and price of food than about politics and religion. Had the economic situation been worse, it is possible that many more peasants would have taken up arms in support of the rebel earls.

The northern uprising acted as a timely reminder to Elizabeth and her government that there were distant regions of the kingdom that had not fully embraced her rule or the changes in religion enacted in the Act of Uniformity 1559. To deal with this, Elizabeth and her ministers adopted a more sensitive attitude to regional issues. They sought out local knowledge and expertise to help them govern proactively. Locally based, landowning **Lord Lieutenants** and Justices of the Peace were employed to supervise the regions on behalf of the Crown. The office of Lord Lieutenant became an important part of local government because these men were entrusted with the defence of the realm. They organised and trained men to defend the kingdom from invasion, as well as keeping the peace alongside JPs.

Social and economic problems

Poverty, vagrancy, unemployment and periodic economic depressions were contributing factors to growing social discontent and protest. Harvest failures and food shortages were an ever-present risk that might lead to rebellion. For example, protest over food shortages and high prices in 1596 culminated in the Oxfordshire rising. To prevent such incidents, Justices of the Peace were given the power to regulate wages, control food prices and, as in the city of Norwich, store grain for times of dearth.

The government took the plight of the poor seriously, and between 1563 and 1601, six major pieces of legislation were passed through parliament to punish the undeserving poor (rogues and vagabonds) and to relieve the deserving poor (the old, the young and the disabled). The more prosperous south-east of England did not suffer as much as the economically deprived midlands and north.

1563	Statute of Artificers
1572	Vagabonds Act
1576	Act for Setting the Poor on Work
1598	Act for the Relief of the Poor
1598	Act for the Punishment of Rogues
1601	Poor Law Act

Quick quizzes at **www.hoddereducation.co.uk/myrevisionnotes**

Turning assertion into argument

Below are a series of definitions, a sample question and two sample conclusions. One of the conclusions achieves a high mark because it contains an argument. The other achieves a lower mark because it contains only description and assertion. Identify which is which. The mark scheme on page 7 will help you.

- **Description:** a detailed account
- **Assertion:** a statement of fact or an opinion which is not supported by a reason
- **Reason:** a statement which explains or justifies something
- **Argument:** an assertion justified with a reason

To what extent did social and economic problems in the regions pose a serious threat to Elizabethan government?

Conclusion 1

> Overall, there is clearly some evidence that the social and economic problems in the regions did pose a serious threat to Elizabethan government. The economically and socially deprived Midlands and north posed the greatest threat to Elizabethan government because they were less prosperous than the south-east of England. Poverty, rising unemployment and periodic economic depressions certainly contributed to growing social discontent and protest. Harvest failures and food shortages led to widespread protest over food prices. The government responded by passing several pieces of legislation through parliament to relieve the deserving poor, such as the old, the young and the disabled. Little was done to help the able-bodied poor.

Conclusion 2

> In conclusion, it is clear that there is sufficient evidence to suggest strongly that the social and economic problems in the regions were so serious that they did indeed pose a threat to Elizabethan government. The government had little to fear in the prosperous south-east of England, where food and work were generally plentiful, but in those regions furthest away from the capital, such as the Midlands and especially the north, the levels of deprivation and desperation were far higher. However, in those regions already suffering from high levels of poverty and vagrancy, harvest failures and food shortages were likely to tip the people into rebellion. For example, a local protest over food shortages and excessive prices turned into a serious rebellion in Oxfordshire in 1596. The government reacted by empowering Justices of the Peace to regulate wages, control food prices and, as in the city of Norwich, store grain for times of dearth.
>
> That the government took the plight of the poor seriously is seen by the fact that between 1563 and 1601, six major pieces of legislation were passed through parliament to punish the undeserving poor (rogues and vagabonds) and to relieve the deserving poor (the old, the young and the disabled).

Recommended reading

Below is a list of suggested further reading on this topic.
- D. Rogerson, S. Ellsmore & D. Hudson, *The Early Tudors: England 1484–1558* (Hodder, 2001)
- J. Lotherington, *The Tudor Years* (Hodder, 1994)
- A. Fletcher & D. MacCulloch, *Tudor Rebellions* (Longman, 1997)

Economic development: trade, exploration and colonisation, prosperity and depression

REVISED

Elizabethan colonial ventures in North America

In 1577, Sir Francis Drake set out to circumnavigate the globe. His aim was twofold: to challenge Spanish dominance of the seas and to seek out new sources of trade. His triumphal return in 1580 can be said to have inaugurated the era of English exploration and colonisation. Inspired by Drake's voyages of discovery, Sir Walter Raleigh persuaded Elizabeth to grant him the authority to seek new lands in North America.

Raleigh and Roanoke

In 1584, Sir Walter Raleigh was granted a royal charter for the colonisation of North America. The aim was to establish territorial rights to a region that had not yet been claimed by Spain. The first colony to be established was at Roanoke Island in 1584. Elizabeth hoped that English colonies in the north of the continent would prove as lucrative as those in the Spanish- and Portuguese-held south. Spain had earned a fortune in gold and silver bullion, which had stimulated its economy and made it the wealthiest kingdom in Europe. Unfortunately for both Raleigh and Elizabeth, the colony established at Roanoke failed to flourish, due in part to the war with Spain and the hostility of local native tribes. Another attempt to establish the colony in 1587 also met with failure.

Overseas trade

One of the most lucrative trades was in slavery. Backed by London merchants, John Hawkins pioneered the slave trade by sailing to Africa in the 1560s, to either capture or purchase slaves. The slaves were then taken to the Caribbean and sold to work on plantations. English merchants sought new markets further afield, and in the 1580s and 1590s trade links were established with India. This led to the formation of the East India Company in 1600.

Economic developments

The scale of economic developments during Elizabeth I's reign can be gauged by the legislation passed through her parliaments. An increasing number of bills were drawn up concerning industries such as the manufacture and trade of cloth, leather, coal and iron. The growth in these industries was encouraged in part by the government, but also by companies and corporations who lobbied for advantageous terms of trade. These lobbyists found a sympathetic ear in Elizabeth's chief minister, Sir William Cecil, who was willing to listen to their proposals. Cecil was well aware that a thriving economy would benefit the kingdom as a whole and help fill the royal treasury with taxes and duties on the manufacture and sale of goods.

Between 1559 and 1563, he steered a series of measures through parliament designed to stimulate the economy. This has been dubbed the 'Elizabethan economic settlement' because it:

- regulated land use for grain and timber, together with measures concerning the export of leather, cloth, coal and iron in English ships
- included the passing of a new Navigation Act and the Statute of Artificers, which sought to encourage apprenticeships and control wages.

Cecil rightly deduced that a healthy economy would promote prosperity, which, in turn, would help establish a peaceful and stable society. Although the government's economic measures could not eliminate periods of depression, they did minimise the potential for protest and rebellion.

Spectrum of importance   a

Below are a sample A-level question and a list of general points which could be used to answer the question. Use your own knowledge and the information on the opposite page to reach a judgement about the importance of these general points to the question posed. Write numbers on the spectrum below to indicate their relative importance. Having done this, write a brief justification of your placement, explaining why some of these factors are more important than others. The resulting diagram could form the basis of an essay plan.

> 'Elizabethan colonial ventures in North America enjoyed significant success.'
>
> Assess the validity of this view.

1 A colony was twice established at Roanoke

2 The colony survived for six years, between 1584 and 1590

3 There had been problems with previous colonial ventures and Spanish opposition

4 This colonial experiment showed that colonisation was possible

5 Future colonists were able to learn from the mistakes made at Roanoke

6 Roanoke paved the way for the successful plantation of Jamestown in Virginia during the reign of James I

← ——————————————————————————————— →

Least important   Most important

Simple essay style

Below is a sample A-level question. Use your own knowledge and the information on the opposite page to produce a plan for this question. Choose four general points, and provide three pieces of specific information to support each general point.

Once you have planned your essay, write the introduction and conclusion for the essay. The introduction should list the points to be discussed in the essay. The conclusion should summarise the key points and justify which point was the most important.

> 'It was Sir William Cecil, Lord Burghley, who was mainly responsible for promoting economic development in Elizabethan England.'
>
> Assess the validity of this view.

Religious developments, change and continuity

Elizabeth and religion

Elizabeth inherited a kingdom in turmoil. While it is possible to trace the changing pattern of official doctrine in the Church of England through the Acts and statutes passed in parliament, this does not reveal what people actually thought. Thirty years of religious change had probably left many people confused and divided. Elizabeth was a Protestant, but in general, it appears that by 1558 the majority of her subjects were still undecided, or fearful of taking sides, about religion.

Support for the Royal Supremacy

There was strong support for the Royal Supremacy among the ruling elite, who were willing to follow the religion of their queen. The mass of the population does not appear to have had strongly held convictions; they simply continued to maintain a conservative affection for the traditional forms of worship, more out of habit than conviction. In fact, in most cases, the commoners were prepared to follow the lead of their social superiors. Although there were small minorities of committed Protestants and Catholics, neither religion seems to have had a strong hold in England when Mary I died.

Puritans and recusants

Although the majority of the population occupied the middle ground between Catholicism and Protestantism, largely ignorant and unsure of which way to turn, on the fringes there were groups of deeply religious people who were committed to either one side or the other. These relatively small groups evolved into the **recusants** and **Puritans** of Elizabeth's later reign. These extremist groups threatened the religious stability of the kingdom, so with unity of the Church in mind, Elizabeth opted for the Religious Settlement enacted in 1559. This settlement kept the peace and lasted the best part of 10 years, but after Elizabeth's excommunication by the Pope in 1570, the Anglican Church became more firmly Protestant. Nonconformity was outlawed, non-attendance at the local parish church was punishable by fine, and persistent offenders were persecuted and imprisoned. Despite this, the Puritan movement continued to grow and evolve, fracturing into rival factions such as the **Presbyterians** and **separatists**. Some Puritan MPs began to agitate for religious change in parliament.

The Counter-Reformation

Elizabeth's largely protestant religious policy fuelled the Counter-Reformation. The Catholic Church tried to counter-attack. Colleges or seminaries were established in Europe to train priests, who were then sent to England to support and spread the Catholic faith. The most famous college was established by exiled English priests at Douai in 1568. Over a hundred priests were sent to England during the 1570s and 1580s, with Catholic literature, to preach and convert. The government not only banned these priests and their books, they also arrested, tortured and executed them. These priests were followed by hard-line Catholics, the **Jesuits**, who were committed to the reconversion of England and who were prepared to die for their faith.

There is no doubt that religious legislation was being enforced in many parishes, but this reveals little about the attitudes of the local people. It might be assumed that, because some parishes had complied with generally unpopular pieces of legislation for setting up communion tables and surrendering church plate, the parishioners were in favour of Protestantism. On the other hand, the record of religious changes might merely indicate that the local authorities were conforming to government policy, and show nothing about popular attitudes.

Spot the mistake

Below are a sample A-level question and an introductory paragraph written in answer to this question. Why does this paragraph not get high praise? What is wrong with the focus of the answer in this paragraph?

'Religion was significantly transformed in the years 1559–85.'

Assess the validity of this view.

> Religion was transformed to a large extent in the period 1559–85 by the Settlement of 1559. Under Elizabeth and her ministers, the government sought to establish a compromise Church that would appeal to both Catholics and Protestants. Thirty years of religious change had probably left many people confused and divided, which is why the queen was determined to resolve the religious question once and for all.

 Developing an argument

Below are a sample question, a list of key points to be made in the essay and a paragraph from the essay. Read the question, the plan and the sample paragraph. Rewrite the paragraph in order to develop an argument. Your paragraph should answer the question directly, and set out the evidence that supports your argument. Crucially, it should develop an argument by setting out a general answer to the question and reasons that support this.

'Elizabeth's religious policy was primarily responsible for the Catholic Counter-Reformation in England in the period 1568–88.'

Assess the validity of this view.

Key points:

- State-sponsored persecution of Catholics was a key feature of government policy.
- Religious conformity was encouraged and penalties for nonconformists were enforced.
- The Catholic Church responded by training priests to re-convert parishioners.
- The Pope excommunicated Elizabeth and declared her a heretic, which encouraged plots.
- Elizabeth tried to avoid persecuting Catholics, but she was driven to it by the threat posed by the Jesuits and seminary priests.

Sample paragraph:

> There is no doubt that Elizabeth's harsh religious policy motivated Catholic activists to plan and execute a counter-reformation in England. Elizabeth's harsh religious policy was a reaction to her excommunication by the Pope in 1570. When the Pope declared Elizabeth a heretic, she became a target for Catholic extremists, who were determined to kill her and replace her with Mary, Queen of Scots. For the first decade of her reign, Elizabeth had tried to steer a middle way between Catholics and Protestants, hoping that a compromise would help keep the peace. However, the papal excommunication not only destroyed the Religious Settlement enacted in 1559, but marked the beginning of the Catholic Counter-Reformation, which included the setting up of colleges or seminaries in Europe to train priests, who were then sent to England to support and spread the Catholic faith. The most famous college was established by exiled English priests at Douai. Several hundred priests were sent to England with Catholic literature to preach and convert. In the face of this challenge, the government felt it had no choice but to adopt a harsh policy. These priests were arrested, tortured and many were executed.

The English renaissance and the 'Golden Age' of art, literature and music

REVISED

The 'Golden Age' of Elizabethan England

Elizabethan England has been described as a 'Golden Age' of art, literature and music because it produced some of the nation's most famous poets, artists, architects and playwrights. This flowering of the English Renaissance was made possible by the generous patronage bestowed by the queen and her courtiers on talented musicians such as William Byrd and artists like Nicholas Hilliard. The generosity displayed at the royal court, the centre of power, set a trend and encouraged members of the titled and landowning elite, the nobility and gentry, to invest in the nation's artistic culture.

Playwrights and poets

Perhaps the most famous member of this cultural movement was the talented playwright and poet William Shakespeare. His poems and plays have endured to this day. Shakespeare was not alone, being joined by such luminaries as Christopher Marlowe and Thomas Dekker. These men were patronised by leading nobles, who formed companies of players who performed their plays at court, as well as in public theatres such as the Globe.

Noble patronage

The Lord Chamberlain's Men was set up in the 1590s under the patronage of the queen's cousin, Henry Carey, Lord Hunsdon. Shakespeare was among those dramatists who wrote for this company. Another leading company was the Lord Admiral's Men, set up in the 1570s under the patronage of Charles Howard, Earl of Nottingham, a cousin of the Howard Dukes of Norfolk.

In some cases, courtiers went further than just patronising skilled musicians and dramatists. For example, Sir Phillip Sidney and Sir Walter Raleigh composed poetry themselves, and their poems rank alongside those by more skilled poets such as Edmund Spenser, whose most famous poem was *The Faerie Queen*. Like Richard Hooker, author of *Laws of Ecclesiastical Polity*, Sidney made significant contributions to literature, being the author of several works such as *Arcadia*.

The spread of learning and literacy

The Renaissance encouraged the spread of learning and literacy. Education was at the forefront of this movement, which explains why so many grammar schools – nearly 30 – were set up during Elizabeth's reign, and why ever greater numbers of students were attending the universities of Oxford and Cambridge. Even members of the nobility began sending their sons to university for a more rounded education, though they were not obliged to obtain a degree. The cultural and intellectual experience of a university education was considered more important than the traditional apprenticeships in the household of a great nobleman. For example, one of Elizabeth's Privy Councillors, Sir John Perrot, had been apprenticed and educated in the household of the Lord Treasurer, William Paulet, Marquis of Winchester. However, when Perrot married and had his own children, he sent them to Oxford University.

How far do you agree?

Read Extract A on the English Renaissance.

Summarise each of the extract's arguments, and use your knowledge to agree or contradict each one.

Arguments in extract	Knowledge that corroborates	Knowledge that contradicts
1		
2		
3		

EXTRACT A

In the first 20 years of the reign of Elizabeth, the poets were all small fry. It took some time for the Elizabethan settlement to take root, for consciousness of nationhood to grow under the threat from Spain, and above all for the new grammar schools, founded after the dissolution of the monasteries, to provide a new educated middle class with literary tastes and ambitions. But the right conditions for literature are useless without men of genius, and Elizabeth's reign saw such men emerge. By the example of Sidney and Spenser, the general level of poetic craftsmanship was immediately raised, and the poets of the last 20 years of Elizabeth's reign, however unequal in ability, could all write competent musical verse.

Adapted from K. Muir, 'Language and Literature', in R. Blake (ed.),
The English World: History, Character and People (Thames and Hudson, 1982)

Simple essay style

Below is a sample question. Use your own knowledge and the information on the opposite page to produce a plan for this question. Choose four general points, and provide three pieces of specific information to support each general point.

Once you have planned your essay, write the introduction and conclusion for it. The introduction should list the points to be discussed in the essay. The conclusion should summarise the key points and justify which point was the most important.

'Later Elizabethan England, c.1580–1603, was a "Golden Age" of art, literature and music.'

Assess the validity of this view.

The last years of Elizabeth: the state of England politically, economically, religiously and socially by 1603

REVISED

Queen Elizabeth

Elizabeth was, arguably, the greatest of the Tudor monarchs. The queen was respected and beloved by her people. She had governed wisely and successfully without a husband, which was no mean feat in a man's world. In partnership with her ministers, Elizabeth had provided stable and effective government and had frustrated the plots and plans of her enemies to remove her from the throne. By 1588, Elizabeth was at the height of her power. She had eliminated her rival, Mary, Queen of Scots, defeated her primary enemy, Philip of Spain and crushed the Catholic threat both at home and abroad. Although some problems still remained – the lack of an heir or named successor, economic difficulties and the enmity of the Pope and Catholic powers – the scene was set for a triumphant end to her reign: this was not to be.

The last decade: repression, rebellion and execution

The last decade of Elizabeth's reign was marked by repression, rebellion and execution.
- An aging queen lacked the energy to control, let alone curb, the rampant ambition of a younger generation of courtiers. Faction fights at court became bitter and divided her courtiers.
- Her peer group, men on whom the queen had long relied for advice and support – Leicester (d.1588) and Burghley (d.1598) – were either dead or dying and could not be easily replaced.
- The Essex rebellion of 1601 was indicative of Elizabeth's decline, both physically and mentally.

Essex had dared to challenge the royal prerogative, but the fact that he had been so easily defeated suggests that the political system was strong and stable enough to cope with the ambition of would-be over-mighty subjects. Elizabethan government was structurally strong, and the administrative system at the centre and in the localities was firm and effective.

Social, economic and religious conditions in England

The peace and stability established during Elizabeth's reign promoted economic growth and social cohesion. Although inflation remained a problem, trade continued to flourish and industry continued to grow. Poverty and vagrancy were social evils which the Crown could not solve, but the passing of a series of parliamentary Acts to provide more relief than punishment was certainly a step in the right direction. Apart from the odd incidence of food riots caused by harvest failures, the general population was seemingly content with their lot.

Religiously, too, the nation had evolved to a point where the majority of the population had come to accept, if not wholeheartedly embrace, the largely Protestant settlement enacted in 1559. By 1603, England was, without doubt, a Protestant kingdom. Catholic and Puritan extremists had been driven to the fringes of society, so that their views did not command the support or respect of the population at large. The Anglican Church was a moderate Protestant institution that had been firmly established by 1603.

Eliminate irrelevance

Below are a sample A-level question and a paragraph written in answer to this question. Read the paragraph and identify parts of the paragraph that are not directly relevant to the question. Draw a line through the information that is irrelevant and justify your deletions in the margin.

> 'The last decade of Elizabeth's reign was mainly one of repression, rebellion and execution.'
>
> Assess the validity of this view.

By the 1590s, Elizabeth was aging, and it showed in her growing inability to control her younger and more energetic courtiers. The court still attracted the ambitious — those who were keen to meet with the queen in the hope of reward. She lost some of her best ministers, such as Burghley and Walsingham, and close friends like Leicester. Elizabeth felt their loss keenly, and it was her search for a replacement in Essex that fanned the flames of revolt. She failed to realise that Essex was overly ambitious, and that unless he was kept under control he could pose a serious threat to her power. Luck, rather than good judgement, saved her from succumbing to Essex's rebellion. His execution was a necessary act of repression because it sent out a powerful warning to those who might challenge the royal prerogative in the future. On the other hand, the twin problems of poverty and vagrancy continued to threaten the social stability of the kingdom. The Spanish were as threatening as ever.

 Develop the detail

Below are a sample A-level question and a paragraph written in answer to this question. The paragraph contains a limited amount of detail.

Annotate the paragraph to add additional detail to the answer.

> 'Elizabeth died unloved and unlamented.'
>
> Assess the validity of this view.

That Elizabeth died unloved and unlamented is not unsurprising, given the longevity of her reign. She had reigned longer than any of her Tudor predecessors and it was the second longest reign since 1066. Elizabeth's obsession with popularity and political security caused her to make many mistakes. Some of these mistakes were so serious that they had the potential to end her rule. Her favourable treatment of the Earl of Essex caused resentment and jealousy at court. Her misjudgement of Essex and her toleration of his aggressively ambitious behaviour was a primary cause of the earl's rebellion in 1601. Elizabeth ended her days as an irritable old woman, presiding over war and failure abroad and poverty and factionalism at home. By the late 1590s, Elizabeth was devoid of any new ideas, and she resorted more and more to ill-temper as a tool of management.

4 The triumph of Elizabeth, 1563–1603

Exam focus

REVISED

Opposite is a sample Level 5 answer on Interpretations. It was written in response to an A-level-style question.

Using your understanding of the historical context, assess how convincing the arguments in these three extracts are in relation to the threat posed to Elizabeth by Mary, Queen of Scots.

EXTRACT A

Mary's arrival set Elizabeth a problem which was only solved nineteen years later by her execution. There were really two Mary Stuarts to be dealt with. One was the sister sovereign in exile, who merited honourable asylum and perhaps assistance to regain her throne. The other was the Catholic claimant to the English succession, if not to the English throne, the woman who would be under Elizabeth – only much more actively and dangerously – what Elizabeth had been under Mary Tudor, and Mary Tudor under Somerset and Northumberland, the magnet drawing together scattered elements of religious and political discontent. How powerful a magnet Mary was, her first 18 months in England amply demonstrated. They saw the first of the reign's conspiracies and its only serious rebellion.

Adapted from S.T. Bindoff,
Tudor England (Penguin, 1952)

EXTRACT B

Elizabeth's attitude towards Mary had always had a schizophrenic twist to it. Fear and distrust of a rival who had asserted her claims from the first days of the reign and had never ceased to pursue them were inherent in their relationship. Elizabeth had not hesitated to checkmate Mary's designs or those of her partisans, by intrigue or by violence when necessary. Everything had been done to taint Mary's reputation, as a party to her husband's murder, as a plotter who intrigued with English rebels and foreign powers, to murder Elizabeth and bring down the English regime. Yet through all the turns and twists of Mary's melodrama, Elizabeth had never lost sight of her sacrosanct status as an anointed monarch, one of God's earthly lieutenants, and above all human judgements.

Adapted from W. MacCaffrey, *Elizabeth I*
(E. Arnold, 1993)

EXTRACT C

Mary in England posed particular problems. Her behaviour in Scotland had not affected her claim to the succession to the throne of England, and her actual presence in England might well loosen the allegiance of Catholics to Elizabeth. It was also conceivable that she would be at the centre of plots to assassinate Elizabeth. After all, assassination on religious grounds was not uncommon in contemporary Europe. Even Mary's implacable opponent Cecil was aware that she had considerable political skill and personal magnetism. Certainly Mary could not be allowed the freedom, at the English court or elsewhere, to build up a faction to support her claim. It seemed, however, that Mary did not need personal freedom to attract support. By 1569, it would appear that some people of great influence were prepared to recognise Mary's position as Elizabeth's heir, providing she were safely married to a suitable Englishman.

Adapted from John Warren, *Elizabeth I: Meeting the Challenge, England,
1541–1603* (Hodder Education, 2008)

These extracts all deal with Mary, Queen of Scots, and they all discuss the reasons why she was such a dangerous threat to Elizabeth. They are all written by historians, which should add weight and authority to what they have to say. As professional historians, their arguments should be convincing, so it is probably fair to say that they will be very useful in understanding the nature and seriousness of the threat Mary posed to her cousin Elizabeth.

The introductory paragraph is not needed in exam conditions. Here it sets the tone of the answer.

Extract A argues that Mary was a serious threat to Elizabeth because after being in England for only a short time, less than 18 months, she had already contributed to 'the first of the reign's conspiracies and its only serious rebellion'. This was the Northern rebellion, when two Catholic earls rebelled against Elizabeth and intended to remove her and put Mary on the throne. This is as serious as it got in the sixteenth century. The extract also suggests that Elizabeth did not quite know what to do with Mary. Elizabeth may also have had some sympathy for Mary, for she, too, had been a prisoner in the reign of Mary I. However, Elizabeth realised that Mary might act as a 'magnet drawing together scattered elements of religious and political discontent'. This is why some of Elizabeth's ministers wanted to execute Mary to prevent her becoming a focus for plots. Elizabeth had herself become the focus of the plans of others when she was unwittingly drawn into the Wyatt rebellion of 1554. Mary had not willingly crossed the border into England; she had been forced to do so. Therefore this extract offers a convincing argument setting out the reasons how and why Mary posed such a threat to Elizabeth. However, the extract does have its limitations, because it says that Mary was 'much more actively and dangerously' involved in plots against Elizabeth, but does not go on to explain this.

This paragraph extends the range of the answer by offering an alternative interpretation to the other two extracts. The author offers a subtle argument that differs markedly from those presented in the other two extracts.

Extract B is very useful and interesting because it is very much more subtle in what it says about the threat posed by Mary, Queen of Scots. It takes a very different approach to either Extract A or C because it says that the threat may not have been as dangerous as was once thought, that it had been deliberately exaggerated by Elizabeth to ruin Mary's reputation. This was a form of propaganda, which was used to provide Elizabeth with the excuse to get rid of Mary. Elizabeth needed an excuse because Mary was, like her, 'an anointed monarch', chosen by God to rule over her people. Since Mary was 'above all human judgements', did Elizabeth and her ministers have the right to detain her, let alone put her on trial and execute her? Some foreign powers did not think so, and nor did many English Catholics. The author of the extract may even be suggesting that Elizabeth provoked Mary into plotting against her. Perhaps Mary was not really a threat to Elizabeth, but was just made to seem as if she was. The arguments presented in this extract are very convincing. Arguably, its only weakness is that it lacks balance, since there is no reference to an alternative view, such as those held by other historians who firmly believe that Mary did pose a threat to Elizabeth.

This paragraph is focused and accurate in its depiction of the argument presented by the author of Extract C. However, the candidate does in part contradict what had been said earlier regarding the subtlety of the argument.

There is no subtlety in Extract C, where the author is quite explicit in stating that Mary not only 'posed particular problems', but that she 'would be at the centre of plots to assassinate Elizabeth'. Clearly, Mary really did pose a serious threat to Elizabeth. It also supports the author of Extract A because it says that she had become the focus of attention. For example, it states that 'Mary did not need personal freedom to attract support' because 'some people of great influence' had already rebelled in 1569. It also suggests that Mary was very dangerous because 'she had considerable political skill and personal magnetism'. Elizabeth's chief minister, Sir William Cecil, recognised the threat that Mary posed, which is why he lobbied Elizabeth to execute her cousin. He finally got his way in 1587. Perhaps this extract is more subtle than one might think on first reading, because it suggests that Mary was not so much a threat to Elizabeth as to Cecil and other ministers like him. He depended on Elizabeth for his office and power, and if she was replaced by Mary, it was likely that he too would have been fired. This had happened to Cecil before, when he held high office under Edward VI, only to be dismissed following Mary I's accession to the throne. Cecil clearly could not face another Mary on the throne! The extract also argues that the real threat to Elizabeth may not have been Mary alone, but other 'suitable Englishmen' like Norfolk, who was involved in a plot to marry Mary. The extract offers a convincing argument, demonstrating the threat Mary posed to Elizabeth.

This is a very good answer. The candidate engages with the question set, and the arguments contained in the extracts are clearly identified. The candidate is clearly aware of the wider context and does attempt to use this knowledge to corroborate and challenge the arguments in appropriate detail. This is a Level 5 response.

Find the evidence

The most important element in producing an argument is supporting evidence and examples. Read the essay again and identify where evidence has been used effectively to support a point.

Timeline

1485	Henry VII's accession to the throne after victory at the battle of Bosworth
1487	Battle of Stoke, ending the Wars of the Roses
1489	Yorkshire rebellion
1497	Cornish rebellion
1499	Execution of the Pretender Perkin Warbeck and Edward, Earl of Warwick
1509	Death of Henry VII; Henry VIII inherits the throne
1511–12	First French War
1514	Thomas Wolsey made Archbishop of York
1515	Wolsey made a Cardinal (November) and appointed Lord Chancellor (December)
1518	Wolsey appointed papal legate
1520	Meeting between Henry VIII and Francis I of France at the Field of the Cloth of Gold
1521	Henry VIII given title of Defender of the Faith by the Pope
1525	Amicable Grant
1526	Eltham Ordinances
1529	Wolsey falls from power; meeting of the Reformation Parliament
1530	Thomas More becomes Lord Chancellor
1532	More resigns as Lord Chancellor; Thomas Cromwell becomes the king's chief adviser
1533	Thomas Cranmer becomes Archbishop of Canterbury
1534	Act of Supremacy passed, severing England's ties with Rome and making Henry VIII head of the Church in England
1536	First Act for the dissolution of the monasteries passed in parliament; Pilgrimage of Grace rebellion breaks out in northern England; Act of Ten Articles
1539	Second Act for the dissolution of the monasteries passed in parliament; execution of Cromwell
1547	Death of Henry VIII; succeeded by Edward VI; government headed by Lord Protector Somerset
1549	Dissolution of the chantries; the Western rebellion (Prayer Book rebellion) and Kett's rebellion break out; Somerset replaced as head of government by Lord President Northumberland; First Book of Common Prayer drawn up and published by Archbishop Cranmer
1552	Second Book of Common Prayer published
1553	Death of Edward VI; succeeded by Mary I after the defeat of the Lady Jane Grey conspiracy
1554	Wyatt rebellion; execution of Northumberland and Lady Jane Grey
1555	Mary restores the Pope as head of the Church
1556	Execution of Archbishop Cranmer; Cardinal Reginald Pole appointed Archbishop of Canterbury
1558	Death of Mary; succeeded by Elizabeth I
1559	Church settlement
1568	Mary, Queen of Scots arrives in England following civil war in Scotland; she is immediately detained
1569	Rebellion of the Northern Earls (Northern rebellion)
1570	Elizabeth excommunicated by the Pope
1571	Ridolfi plot
1583	Throckmorton plot
1586	Babington plot
1587	Mary, Queen of Scots executed
1588	Spanish Armada
1601	Essex rebellion
1603	Death of Elizabeth I

Glossary

Act of Attainder Act passed through parliament declaring the accused guilty with no need for a trial.

Act of Supremacy Act passed through parliament in 1534, recognising Henry VIII as head of the Church in England. Another Act was passed in 1559, by which Elizabeth became Supreme Governor of the Church.

Act of Uniformity Act passed through parliament enforcing religious conformity.

Acts of Union Acts passed through parliament uniting Wales with England, politically, legally and administratively.

Amicable Grant Tax imposed by Lord Chancellor Wolsey. In spite of its name, it was essentially a forced loan.

Anticlericalism Opposition to or criticism of the Church and the clergy.

Babington plot Plot hatched by Sir Anthony Babington to assassinate Elizabeth I and replace her with Mary, Queen of Scots.

Bonds and recognisances Bonds: written contracts or agreements of good behaviour. Recognisances: public acknowledgements of actual debts and other obligations owed to the Crown.

Bosworth Battle fought in Leicestershire on 22 August 1485, between the Lancastrian claimant, Henry Tudor, and the Yorkist king, Richard III.

Burgess Man of business, owning property in towns and serving on the ruling council or in municipal office.

Calvinist Follower of John Calvin, an influential French theologian who helped to progress the Protestant Reformation in Europe after Luther.

Collectanea satis copiosa ('the sufficiently large collection') Compiled by Cranmer to add intellectual authority to the king's case in seeking an annulment of his marriage.

Consubstantiation Protestant belief that the bread and wine of Communion only represent the flesh and blood of Christ spiritually.

Convocation Ruling council of the Church, a form of parliament.

Copyhold Land held according to the feudal custom of the manor, where the title deed received by the tenant was a copy of the relevant entry in the manorial court roll.

Council Learned in the Law Responsible for marriage, wardship and relief of all the king's tenants and the collection of feudal dues.

County Palatine Secular and/or ecclesiastical lordships ruled by noblemen or bishops, possessing special authority and autonomy from the rest of a kingdom.

Courts of assize Senior courts in each county, presided over by a judge appointed by the Crown.

Court of General Surveyors Government department responsible for auditing the revenues from Crown lands.

Court of king's Bench Senior criminal court based in London.

Customary tenures Traditional forms of landholding dating back to the feudal system.

Debasement of the coinage Means whereby the government tried to save money by reducing the content of gold and silver in coins and replacing them with cheaper metals, such as copper, which lowered the value of the currency.

Device Method by which the succession was determined.

Distraint of knighthood Feudal law forcing landholders with annual incomes of £20 to accept knighthoods.

Edwardian Prayer Books of 1549 and 1552 Protestant Prayer Books used in Church services, first issued in 1549 and extensively revised in 1552; they were further revised in 1559.

Elizabethan Church Settlement Acts passed through parliament establishing the Anglican Church and rules of worship.

Eltham Ordinances Wolsey's attempt to reform the king's Household in 1526.

Enclosure Enclosing of land with hedges or fences to make it easier to raise livestock.

Eucharist A rite or sacrament known as Holy Communion which celebrates the Lord's Supper.

Excommunication Expulsion or banishment of a person from the Church. An excommunicant could no longer worship, marry or be buried in church.

Feudal dues Traditional customs, such as marriage payments or inheritance tax, associated with the feudal system.

Feudal system Medieval system of landholding and obligations of service.

Field of the Cloth of Gold Venue in northern France for a grand meeting between Henry VIII of England and Francis I of France, 7–24 June 1520.

Forty-Two Articles Drawn up by Thomas Cranmer as a summary of Anglican doctrine in the Protestant faith in the reign of Edward VI.

Great Chain of Being Social pyramid showing everyone's place in society, as decreed by God.

Habsburgs Family name of the ruling dynasty that reigned in sixteenth-century Spain, Austria, the Netherlands and the Holy Roman Empire.

Hanseatic League Merchants from the mainly German city ports on the Baltic Sea who came together to form a trading union.

Heretical Religious nonconformists who reject the teachings and rules of the Catholic Church.

Holy Roman Empire Large, central European state, roughly equivalent to modern Germany, ruled by an elected emperor.

Intercursus Magnus Commercial treaty signed in 1496 by Henry VII of England and Philip IV, Duke of Burgundy.

Intercursus Malus ('evil treaty') Name given by the Dutch to the treaty passed in 1507 that was intended to replace the *Intercursus Magnus*, the commercial treaty which the Dutch thought was far too favourable to English interests.

Jesuits Members of the Society of Jesus, set up in 1540 by the Catholic Church to reconvert Protestants and eliminate Protestantism in Europe.

Justice of the Peace Royal officer responsible for government, administration and justice at county level.

Justification by faith Proof of belief by faith alone, without having to prove loyalty by good works or deeds.

King's writ did not run Semi-independent lordships where the king's written orders were not recognised and had no force in law.

King's council Council consisting of the king's closest advisers.

Labour services Feudal obligation by tenants to work on their landlord's lands.

Legatine court Court set up in specific countries carrying the full authority of the Pope to determine legal cases.

Livery and maintenance Uniforms and badges worn by retainers who serve their lords.

Lollardy Religious movement that existed from the mid-fourteenth century to the English Reformation. The Catholic Church regarded its members, Lollards, as being heretics.

Lord Chancellor Highest legal and administrative office in the English government, often equated with being the monarch's chief minister.

Lord Lieutenant Military officer appointed to a county, concerned with the training of troops and the defence of the realm.

Lord Protector Legal title given to senior nobleman appointed to govern the kingdom on behalf of a child monarch.

Lutheran Followers and faith of Martin Luther.

Marcher lordships Semi-independent lordships in Wales and the border region, ruled by noblemen possessing special authority from the Crown.

Merchant Adventurers Company of English merchants who traded with the Netherlands and north-west Germany, principally in the export of finished cloth.

Navigation Acts Acts passed through parliament in an attempt to promote and protect English trade and thereby break the monopoly enjoyed by the Hanseatic League.

Papal bull Act passed by a Pope, and a legally binding document issued to specific countries.

Papal legate Representative of the Pope, given full papal powers in a specific country.

Pastoral duties Work of the parish priest, such as baptism, marriage and burial.

Penance Sacrament of penance involved the repentance of sins by means of confession.

Pilgrimage of Grace Rebellion in the north of England, 1536–37.

Praemunire Law prohibiting the assertion or maintenance of papal jurisdiction in England and preventing English clerics from appealing to Rome.

Presbyterians Puritan members of the Anglican Church who wished to reform the state Church from within.

Privy Councillors Senior government ministers who met with and advised the monarch in a private ruling council. They managed the government of the kingdom on behalf of the monarch.

Prorogue Temporary suspension of parliament.

Puritans Radical Protestants who reject all Catholic practices in church worship.

Quarter sessions   Courts held four times a year in every county and presided over by JPs.

Recusants   Catholics in Elizabethan England who remained loyal to the Pope and refused to conform to the state religion.

Regent   Person who governs the country on behalf of the monarch.

Reformation Parliament   Parliament that met between 1529 and 1536 and transformed the Church by breaking from Rome and making Henry VIII Supreme Head of the Church in England.

Regular clergy   Monks and nuns who lived and worshipped in monastic institutions.

Renaissance   Flowering of knowledge in the late fifteenth and sixteenth centuries, focusing on science, art and classical civilisation.

Retaining   Medieval system whereby great lords recruited those of a lower social status as their followers or servants.

Royal prerogative   Rights and privileges that traditionally belonged to the monarch, such as making war, peace and marriage.

Secular clergy   Priests and chaplains who lived and worshipped in the community and led services in the local parish church.

Separatists   Hard-line Puritans who split from the Presbyterian movement to set up their own religious group, which was entirely independent of the Anglican Church.

Serfdom   Serfs were the lowest social class of feudal society, with few rights.

Star Chamber   The Court of Star Chamber dealt with serious crimes, both civil and criminal. It was especially effective in dealing with the nobility and gentry.

Statute of Uses 1535–36   Law designed to prevent landowners transferring land to third parties, which meant that the Crown could not tax it because it was being used by people other than the person who owned it.

Subsidy Act 1534   Cromwell's attempt to raise money by assessing the value of a person's goods. It was opposed because it was levied in peacetime.

Supplication against the Ordinaries   List of clerical abuses that Henry VIII intended to reform.

Thirty-Nine Articles   Defining statements of doctrines of the Church of England, setting out acts of worship in church services in the reign of Elizabeth I.

Transubstantiation   Catholic belief that the bread and wine offered in the celebration of the sacrament of the Eucharist become, in reality, the body and blood of Jesus Christ.

Wardship   Medieval system whereby a child is made a ward of the Crown, which then takes care of the child until he or she reaches the legal age to inherit lands.

Yeomen   Social class of richer peasants, who may have been as wealthy as some of the gentry, but were below them in social class.

Key figures

Anne Boleyn (d.1536) Second wife of Henry VIII, faction leader and one of the main causes of the break with Rome.

John Calvin (d.1564) Influential French theologian who established himself at Geneva, where he helped to progress the Protestant Reformation in Europe.

Campeggio (d.1539) Italian cardinal and papal legate sent to preside over Henry VIII's divorce from Catherine of Aragon.

Catherine of Aragon (d.1536) Daughter of Ferdinand and Isabella of Spain. Married Henry VII's son, Prince Arthur, in 1501, but following his death she married Henry VIII, in 1509.

William Cecil, Lord Burghley (d.1598) Secretary of State in Edward VI's reign and chief minister during the reign of Elizabeth. He was one of the most powerful men in English politics.

Clement VII (d.1534) Pope who refused to grant Henry VIII's annulment of his marriage.

John Colet (d.1519) Churchman, humanist scholar, teacher and educational pioneer.

Thomas Cranmer (d.1556) Cleric and scholar who became Archbishop of Canterbury. He led the Reformation in England. He was executed for his Protestant faith by Mary I.

Thomas Cromwell (d.1540) Trained lawyer who served Cardinal Wolsey as his chief adviser and then Henry VIII as his chief minister.

Edmund Dudley (d.1510) Minister responsible for tax collection in Henry VII's government, executed by Henry VIII.

Robert Dudley, Earl of Leicester (d.1588) Son of John Dudley, Duke of Northumberland, he became one of Elizabeth's closest friends and adviser. He was a member of the Privy Council and one of the most influential men in English politics.

Edward, Earl of Warwick (d.1499) Nephew of Edward IV and Richard III, who was kept as a prisoner as a child. He was executed, years later, for plotting with Warbeck against Henry VII.

Richard Empson (d.1510) Minister responsible for the Council Learned in the Law in Henry VII's government, executed by Henry VIII.

Desiderius Erasmus (d.1536) Churchman from the Netherlands and one of the most famous humanist scholars of his generation.

John Fisher (d.1535) English bishop and humanist scholar who opposed Henry VIII's annulment, his marriage with Anne Boleyn and the break with Rome. Executed in 1535.

Richard Fox (d.1528) English bishop who served as a minister in the reigns of Henry VII and Henry VIII. His area of expertise was foreign affairs.

Stephen Gardiner (d.1555) English bishop who led the conservative faction at court during the reigns of Henry VIII and Edward VI. He was imprisoned by Edward VI, but released by Mary I, whom he served as a government minister.

Thomas Howard, Duke of Norfolk (d.1554) Powerful nobleman who served on Henry VIII's council and led the conservative faction at court. Retired from politics during Edward VI's reign, but served on Mary's council.

Hugh Latimer (d.1555) English bishop and humanist scholar who was burned as a heretic by Mary I.

Martin Luther (d.1546) German monk and theologian who began the Reformation in Europe. He established the Lutheran Church and became an enemy of the Pope and the Catholic Church.

Thomas More (d.1535) Lawyer and humanist scholar who became Henry VIII's Lord Chancellor in 1530. He resigned in 1532 and refused to accept Henry as head of the Church, for which he was executed.

John Morton (d.1500) Archbishop of Canterbury, Cardinal and Lord Chancellor of England. He was one of Henry VII's closest and most powerful advisers.

John de la Pole, Earl of Lincoln (d.1487) Nephew of Edward IV and Richard III, he was a leader of the Yorkists after the death of Richard III and was killed at the battle of Stoke.

Simon Renard (d.1573) Spanish ambassador to England who served as one of Mary I's closest advisers.

Lambert Simnel (d.c.1535) Impostor from a humble background who pretended to be the nephew of Edward IV. He was a figurehead for dissident Yorkists seeking to topple Henry VII. He was pardoned and served in the king's Household.

Perkin Warbeck (d.1499) Impostor from a humble background who pretended to be the younger son of Edward IV. A figurehead for dissident Yorkists seeking to topple Henry VII.

Thomas Wolsey (d.1530) Powerful churchman who held various offices of Church and State. He was Henry VIII's chief minister for 15 years.

Answers

Section 1: Henry VII, 1485–1509

Page 9, Spot the mistake

This does not get to a Level 3 because the answer is too simplistic – 'his father was an earl and not a king', or 'His grandfather was not even an Englishman, he was a Welsh squire' – and not fully focused on the key part of the question, 'To what extent'. The answer should offer a counter-argument by highlighting the strengths of Henry's claims to the throne.

Page 9, Support or challenge?

The following statements support:
- Henry VII was descended from Edward III
- Henry VII was the half-nephew of Henry VI
- Henry VII married Elizabeth, the daughter of Edward IV

The following statements challenge:
- Henry VII was a hard-working and energetic monarch
- Henry VII had the support of the Pope and the Church
- Henry VII controlled the nobility

Page 11, Spectrum of importance

Most important:
- 1 Work and advice of the elite group of councillors in the king's Council
- 2 The effectiveness of the Council Learned in the Law
- 6 Henry VII

Least important:
- 3 The key men entrusted with responsibility for the regional councils
- 4 The work of the sheriffs and the Justices of the Peace
- 5 Bonds and recognisances and laws against retaining

Page 13, Spot the mistake

This does not get to a Level 3 because it lacks substantive detail. The answer is too general – 'he ruthlessly exploited and developed the kingdom's revenue system' – and lacks examples or explanation.

Page 13, Interpretations: content or argument?

Answer 1 focuses on content, whereas Answer 2 focuses on argument.

Page 15, RAG – rate the timeline

1487	Margaret, Duchess of Burgundy, supports Lambert Simnel's rebellion with troops and money
1489	Henry signs the Treaty of Redon
1489	England and Spain agree to the terms in the Treaty of Medina del Campo
1492	The Treaty of Étaples is concluded between France and England
1493	Henry breaks off trade relations with Burgundy because of Margaret, Duchess of Burgundy's support for Perkin Warbeck
1495	James IV of Scotland offers to support Warbeck
1497	The Truce of Ayton is agreed between England and Scotland
1502	The Treaty of Ayton is signed

1503   The Treaty of Ayton is sealed by the marriage of king James IV of Scotland to Henry VII's daughter, Margaret

1503   Burgundy ceases to be a threat after the death of Margaret, Duchess of Burgundy

1508   Henry achieves a measure of stability in his foreign relations and his position on the throne is secure from foreign intervention

Page 17, Delete as applicable

Henry VII was successful in securing the succession to a **great** extent. In this way, Henry VII's attempt to secure the succession was **extremely** successful because he established secure foundations for a dynasty that survived for more than a century.

Page 17, RAG – rate the interpretation

Henry's foreign policy illustrates his realism and lack of illusion. Where Edward IV had harboured delusions of re-conquering France, Henry VII pursued a limited policy based on peace with France and alliance with Spain; this enabled him gradually to eliminate the risk of conspiracies against the throne launched from overseas.

Henry VII acted with energy and decisiveness in his dealings with all rivals of royal blood. Edward IV had attempted to buy off potential rivals with grants of land and office. Henry, in contrast, tried to neutralise any rivals before they could be used as figureheads by conspirators.

Henry's success in dealing with conspiracies owed much to the conspirators, but also reflected his persistence and ruthlessness. The best means of further strengthening his dynasty was by eliminating potential foreign supporters of pretenders and concluding favourable marriage alliances for his family. For these reasons, a realistic and successful foreign policy was essential for the security of his dynasty.

Henry was obsessed with the need to preserve order and retain the loyalty of his subjects. Indeed, it is in this area that Henry was seen at his most ruthless, and his methods were certainly controversial and unpopular. But, like all successful rulers, Henry also enjoyed good fortune.

Page 19, Summarise the arguments

As society grew, differences between one class and another narrowed. The sixteenth century saw the rise of the gentry class. The expansion of this group helped to cause an obsession with the symbols of rank, as those with traditional status tried to protect their elite position.

Page 19, Eliminate irrelevance

~~Early modern English society was structured and governed by strict rules so that everyone knew his or her place. The Church taught that God was responsible for these rules which were explained in the so-called 'Great Chain of Being'.~~ The different ranks in society were determined by title, wealth and breeding, which made it virtually impossible for members of the lowest rank, the commoners, to improve their social status. ~~However, by developing the economy and promoting the increase in trade~~, Henry VII provided the means by which enterprising members of the commons could make a fortune. For example, Robert Wolsey, a butcher ~~and cattle dealer from Ipswich~~, used his wealth ~~by trade~~ to educate and promote the ecclesiastical career of his son, Thomas. Thomas entered the service of Bishop Richard Fox, where he learnt the art of government and administration. Thomas later became Lord Chancellor and one of the most powerful men in England under Henry VIII.

(The statements are too general and do not add to or enhance the answer. They are simply pieces of additional information.)

Page 23, Spot the mistake

This does not get to a Level 3 because the answer is too general. For example, there is a reference to 'the Navigation Acts', but it is not developed or explained. Similarly, general statements, such as 'maritime trade was encouraged and developed', are left unexplained. Why did the 'trade embargo' lead 'to a severe depression in the cloth industry'?

Page 25, Support or challenge?

The following statements support:
- The invention of the printing press and its arrival in England
- The spread of literacy
- The Church supported the Crown

The following statements challenge:
- The influence of the Renaissance
- Henry VII suppressed Lollardy and anticlericalism
- The development of a humanist circle at the royal court

Page 31, Delete as applicable

Henry VIII's attempt to build upon and honour his father's legacy was successful to a **great** extent. In this way, Henry's attempt to address his father's legacy was **extremely** successful because he built upon the secure foundations established by his father to consolidate and enhance the power of the monarchy.

Section 2: Henry VIII and the Royal Supremacy, 1509–47

Page 33, Turning assertion into argument

The first conclusion is mainly description and assertion.

The second conclusion would gain a higher mark because it contains reason and argument.

Page 33, Moving from assertion to argument

There were some changes in Henrician government in the years 1515–40 because Henry VIII was not prepared to work long hours and deal with the details of government business. He preferred to employ talented and energetic chief ministers, whom he entrusted with the government and administration of the kingdom.

Page 35, Spot the mistake

This does not get to a Level 3 because the answer does not offer an explanation, it is merely description. The answer should offer a counter-argument by highlighting the areas that were less successful in changing or transforming the government.

Page 35, Support or challenge?

The following statements support:
- The Amicable Grant was an innovation in the assessment and collection of taxes
- Government became increasingly centralised under Henry VIII
- The unification of Church and state made Henry the most powerful monarch in English history
- Henry VIII was more successful in raising revenue

The following statements challenge:
- Henry VIII governed the kingdom through specially appointed chief ministers
- Henry VII was more successful in securing the succession
- Henry VII dominated the day-to-day running of royal government

Page 39, Interpretations: content or argument?

Answer 1 focuses on content, whereas Answer 2 focuses on argument.

Page 41, RAG – rate the timeline

1415	Battle of Agincourt
1489	Treaty of Medina del Campo
1512	Campaign in Gascony
1513	Battle of Flodden
1513	Battle of the Spurs

Quick quizzes at **www.hoddereducation.co.uk/myrevisionnotes**

1518	Treaty of London
1520	Field of the Cloth of Gold
1522–25	French campaign
1542	Battle of Solway Moss
1544	Capture of the port of Boulogne
1544–46	French campaign

Page 43, Support or challenge?

The following statements support:
- The sale and leasing out of the great estates created a very active land market
- The urban elite enjoyed an unprecedented rise in their status, wealth and power
- The peasantry were now free and could move about the country more freely
- Merchants, retailers and craftsmen were returned to parliament in increasing numbers
- The redistribution of land marked the beginning of the rise of the gentry

The following statements challenge:
- The social structure had altered very little
- Tudor society was still overwhelmingly rural, and retained many of the characteristics of the old feudal system

Page 47, Eliminate irrelevance

There is little doubt that the rapid rise in inflation during the reign of Henry VIII was one among a number of factors that had a significant impact on the lives of the people. Prices and rents continued to rise steadily after 1509, and by the 1530s grain and meat prices had doubled. This was due in part to the poor harvests of the 1520s, but even after a run of good harvests prices showed no sign of falling. ~~Merchants and landowners were determined to increase their profits — hence the failure to reduce prices.~~ Other equally important factors that contributed to the economic development of the kingdom included the debasement of the coinage ~~and the introduction of new techniques, crops and methods of field rotation in the agricultural industry.~~ These factors had a profound effect on the lives of the people.

(The deleted sections are merely description and do not add anything that specifically addresses the question.)

Page 49, Spectrum of importance

Most important:
- 5 The dissolution of the monasteries
- 6 The effects of price rises, inflation and unemployment
- 1 Parliamentary legislation on taxation

Least important:
- 2 Political conflict at court

Page 57, Spot the mistake

This does not get to a Level 3 because it simply describes events and does not directly address the question.

Section 3: Instability and consolidation: the 'mid-Tudor crisis', 1547–63

Page 61, Delete as applicable

Edward VI's foreign policy was successful to a **fair** extent. In this way, Edward's foreign policy was **moderately** successful because it continued the status quo without developing a policy unique to his reign. The aim seems to have been to avoid war rather than forge new alliances and conclude new treaties.

Page 63, Spot the mistake

This does not get to a Level 3 because it mainly describes events, with only a single attempt to offer a supporting example – 'The printing press enabled them to publish theological literature which was used to underpin the work of hard-working preachers.'

Page 65, Spectrum of importance

Most important:
- 1 Policy and impact of the enclosing of land
- 4 Decline and depression in the cloth trade
- 5 Radical Protestant religious reforms
- 3 Religious turmoil and economic difficulties inherited from Henry VIII

Least important:
- 2 Division and political rivalry at court
- 6 Breakdown in the notion and principles of the Great Chain of Being

Page 67, RAG – rate the interpretation

On the eve of her succession, Mary Tudor was in many ways old at 37, certainly embittered and otherwise fatally influenced by her peculiar apprenticeship. Not surprisingly, she would prove a distrustful queen. Having been rejected by or separated from those to whom she would normally have felt closest, she came to place her faith in ideals rather than in people. Chief among such ideals was her desire to marry, and perhaps to know as a wife and mother that domestic felicity of which she had been deprived in her own adolescence. Finally, and obviously linked to these other considerations, came her preference for and trust in Spaniards, who had ever been her aid and comfort, rather than Englishmen.

Page 69, Eliminate irrelevance

In some respects, it is fair to say that the Crown's foreign policy was responsible for the outbreak of serious unrest in England. For example, Henry VIII's break with Rome and his snubbing of Spain by annulling his marriage to the popular Catherine of Aragon led to a rebellion in the north of England. Later in the period, people feared that Mary I, as the first female ruling monarch, would be dominated by her Spanish husband and his male advisers. ~~Her age was another factor. At 37, Mary was quite old for her first marriage, and~~ it was feared that childbirth might result in her death. ~~Childbirth was the biggest killer of women in the sixteenth century.~~ The political elite feared another minority should Mary die and leave a baby as heir. ~~The birth of a child would further endanger Elizabeth's life.~~ As the focus of Protestant hopes for a return to the faith of her brother, Edward VI, Elizabeth posed a threat to Mary.

(The deleted section deviates from the question and overcomplicates matters by hypothesising.)

Page 75, Interpretations: content or argument?

Answer 1 focuses more on the content.

Answer 2 focuses more on the arguments.

The first answer simply describes events – 'This extract states' – whereas the second extract attempts to debate the issues – 'This extract argues'.

Section 4: The triumph of Elizabeth, 1563–1603

Page 81, Eliminate irrelevance

Political competition, allied to personal ambition, lay at the heart of the factional rivalry that caused serious difficulties at court. The two most powerful members of the court were the queen's favourites, Robert Dudley, Earl of Leicester (from 1564) and William Cecil, Lord Burghley (from 1571). ~~They became rivals in government, with each striving to outdo the other in terms of attracting the queen's attention.~~ As high-ranking courtiers in receipt of royal patronage, they naturally attracted powerful supporters. Some of these supporters or clients ~~were based at court,~~

while others exercised their authority in the regions. ~~Their disagreements over government policy often led to stalemate, with the result that some key decisions and some vital pieces of legislation were either delayed or abandoned.~~ This struggle for dominance in the Council sometimes disrupted the smooth running of government.

(The answer veers into description and deals only with two faction rivals, without reference to other powerful courtiers or faction leaders. The extract is generalised and does not make it clear if the rivalry was a serious problem throughout Elizabeth's reign. Some statements – 'Their disagreements over government policy often led to stalemate, with the result that some key decisions and some vital pieces of legislation were either delayed or abandoned' – require examples and/or further explanation.)

Page 81, RAG – rate the interpretation

The rebellion of the Earl of Essex is perhaps the clearest sign of a decline in Elizabeth herself. Until now, her favourites had been devoted to their queen. **No one dared to rebel.** Essex, although he was the poorest earl in England, was related to Elizabeth, for he was descended from her aunt, Mary Boleyn. More importantly, he was Leicester's stepson and had been brought up in Burghley's household. Such advantages gave Essex a head start over other courtiers, but it was his personality that secured his pre-eminence. Essex's relationship with Elizabeth was also stormy. In 1587, Essex accused Elizabeth of taking orders from Raleigh. Thus the story of Elizabeth and Essex was, from the beginning, one of quarrels, confrontations, rebukes and forgiveness. Essex did not perhaps fully understand the queen, underrating her experience and intellect, and did not appreciate that there were limits to the behaviour of even a royal favourite. The fact that Essex was also highly popular with the public did nothing to quell his ambition. Earlier favourites, including Leicester, had been unpopular, disliked because of their presumed ambition. Politically, Essex appeared to be playing a key role. Elizabeth had never allowed one man or faction to create rivalries that disrupted her court or council.

Page 83, Introducing and concluding an argument

Introduction:

The introduction is focused on the question and provides a meaningful guide to the direction the essay intends to take. It suggests that the issue is a matter for debate and that there are two sides to the argument. In short, this is a very good introduction.

Conclusion:

The conclusion is short and could be expanded to summarise the key findings in the essay. Although the final statement is worthy, it does not address the question directly because it does not say whether the plots were a consistent feature of Elizabeth's reign or not. A reference to the fact that there were at least five plots – giving the dates – would help to answer the key phrase in the question by suggesting that they were a consistent feature for only part of her reign – a 15-year period between 1571 and 1586, in a 45-year reign.

Page 85, Support or challenge?

The following statements support:
- The landed elite feared disorder and protest because they might lead to rebellion
- Sixty per cent of the population lived at or below the poverty line
- There was widespread belief that men without masters were inclined to commit crime

The following statements challenge:
- The maintenance of public order was the prime responsibility of Tudor government
- The wealth of the urban elite had increased substantially
- Social mobility gradually turned into social integration through marriage

Page 85, Spectrum of importance

Most important:
- 1 The Edwardian Vagrancy Act, 1547
- 5 Parliamentary Acts of 1598 and 1601 and the setting up of a system of poor relief

- 2 The Statute of Artificers, 1563
- 3 Fear of widespread crime, disorder and protest

Least important:
- 6 Breakdown in the notion and principles of the Great Chain of Being
- 4 The role of the Church

Arguably, the two most important points are 1 and 5, because they highlight the scale of the change in attitude over a period of half a century, between 1547 and 1601. Point 3 acts as a signpost to the changing attitude of the authorities on how to deal with the poor and vagrant.

Page 89, Spectrum of importance

Most important:
- 6 Roanoke paved the way for the successful plantation of Jamestown in Virginia during the reign of James I
- 5 Future colonists were able to learn from the mistakes made at Roanoke
- 1 A colony was twice established at Roanoke
- 4 This colonial experiment showed that colonisation was possible

Least important:
- 2 The colony survived for six years, between 1584 and 1590
- 3 There had been problems with previous colonial ventures and Spanish opposition

Points 6 and 5 are the most important because they deal with colonial ventures as a whole, whereas points 1 and 4 offer a counter-argument, suggesting that colonial ventures did not enjoy significant success.

Page 91, Spot the mistake

This does not get to a Level 3 because the answer does not directly address the key phrase 'significantly transformed'. The impact of the 1559 Settlement needs to be clearly stated.

Page 95, Eliminate irrelevance

By the 1590s, Elizabeth was aging and it showed in her growing inability to control her younger and more energetic courtiers. ~~The court still attracted the ambitious – those who were keen to meet with the queen in the hope of reward.~~ She lost some of her best ministers, such as Burghley and Walsingham, and close friends like Leicester. Elizabeth felt their loss keenly, and it was her search for a replacement in Essex that fanned the flames of revolt. She failed to realise that Essex was overly ambitious, and that unless he was kept under control he could pose a serious threat to her power. ~~Luck, rather than good judgement, saved her from succumbing to Essex's rebellion.~~ His execution was a necessary act of repression because it sent out a powerful warning to those who might challenge the royal prerogative in the future. ~~On the other hand, the twin problems of poverty and vagrancy continued to threaten the social stability of the kingdom. The Spanish were as threatening as ever.~~

(The deleted sections are mainly descriptive detail that does not directly focus on the question.)

Notes

Notes